CUB SCOUT

MAGIC BOOK

SCOUT MAGIC

by Francis J. Rigney

Member, Society of American Magicians

Illustrated by the author

BOY SCOUTS OF AMERICA
IRVING, TEXAS

1990 Printing
Copyright 1960
BOY SCOUTS OF AMERICA
Irving, Texas
Library of Congress Catalog Card Number: 68-9495
ISBN 0-8395-3219-9
No. 3219   Printed in U.S.A.

CONTENTS

FOREWORD

WHEN I was a boy a magician took from my pockets things that I knew could not have been there. I found a small book on magic that told me how the trick was done and soon I was magically finding things in other people's pockets.

Before long I met others who like myself liked magic and I joined them in the Society of American Magicians, which includes both professional magicians and amateurs.

During the years when I was an artist on the BOYS' LIFE staff, I had many opportunities to put on shows of magic and sleight of hand. These were always a lot of fun, but it is just as much fun to do a few tricks that amaze your friends.

If you learn some of the tricks in this book, you can have a wonderful time with them, and who knows, you may become a magician!

FRANCIS J. RIGNEY

Tricks and Puzzles
with Matches

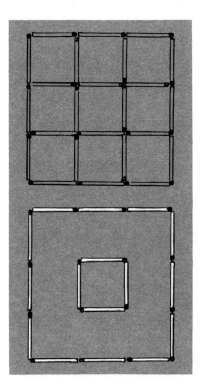

ALTHOUGH the instructions that follow call for matches, a number of the tricks and puzzles can be done with lollipop sticks, soda straws, toothpicks, or small straight twigs. If you decide on matches, use the large kitchen-size ones.

In most of these tricks and puzzles you make a certain number of squares or triangles with the matches and then, by taking some away or moving some to new positions you change the number of squares or triangles.

The drawings show how to start and also how to do each puzzle.

With twenty-four matches make nine squares. Ask your friends to take away eight matches and leave only two squares. Let them try to do this a few times before you show them how. The second picture shows how the puzzle is done.

In the drawings the X's mark the matches to move and where to put them back.

Five Squares to Four

Place sixteen matches to make five squares. Move and put back two to make four squares.

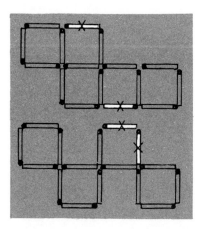

Four Squares to Three

Place twelve matches to make four squares. Move and put back three to make three squares.

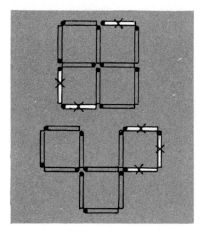

Four Squares to Three

Move four and put back four matches to make three squares.

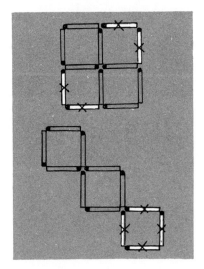

Five Squares to Four

Place fifteen matches to make five squares. Move and put back three to make four squares.

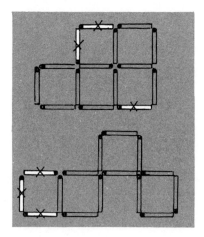

REMOVING MATCHES

Nine Squares to Five Squares

How to take four matches from nine squares so as to leave five squares. The marked matches are the ones to be taken.

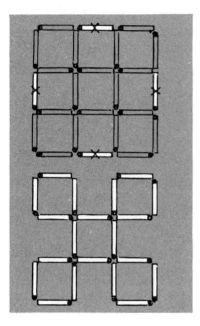

Match Puzzle Contests

Give each person a set of matches. Conduct contests to see who can solve the puzzles first.

Four Squares to Two

How to take two matches from four squares so as to leave two squares. A corner square like the one shown here can be left by taking away ten matches in the nine-square puzzle.

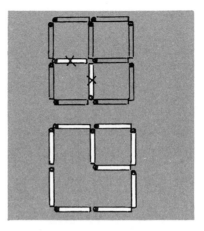

Six Triangles to Three Triangles

How to take three matches from six triangles made with twelve matches to leave three triangles.

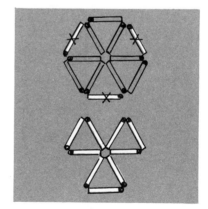

Six Triangles to Four

How to move and put back six matches to make four triangles is shown at the top of page 4.

3

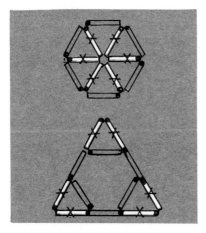

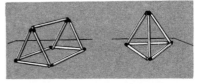

MAKING SQUARES AND TRIANGLES

Give each of your friends eight matches. First ask them to make three squares, then two squares and four triangles, and then two squares and eight triangles. Wait until they have tried a few times to do each puzzle before you show how to do it. The pictures below show you how.

TWO MATCHES, ONE SQUARE

Secretly prepare two matches by bending them in half. They will break but must not be broken apart. Hold the matches between thumb and first finger as shown so that the bent parts cannot be seen and so that your friends will think that they are looking at two straight matches.

Tell them that you can make a square with the two matches. The picture shows how it is done.

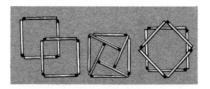

Next, give each friend an extra match and ask that he make three squares and two triangles with the nine matches. How to do this and how to make four triangles with six matches is shown above. You will have to practice to get the matches to stay in position.

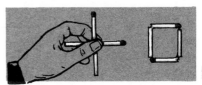

Hide the best matches for this trick in your pocket while doing other tricks with matches on the table. When ready to make the square, gather the table matches with one hand as you take the bent ones from your pocket with the other hand. Be sure you are not seen combining the bent matches with the table matches that the free hand covers. It will now be easy to place the bent matches secretly between the thumb and finger.

ARITHMETIC WITH MATCHES

Six Matches with Five Added

Ask your friends how much five added to six will make. When you are told eleven, say that you will add five matches to six and make nine. Below you see how to do it.

Four Matches with Five Added

How to add five to four and make ten.

Addition and Subtraction

Here the picture shows how to add five of ten matches to make four-

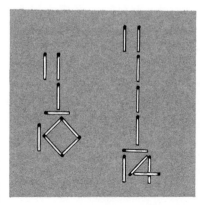

teen and how to subtract one from two to get ten. Give each friend ten matches and ask him to do these problems. After a few minutes show how it can be done easily.

Multiplication

Now, ask that any two odd numbers be taken and multiplied to make seven. Few people will think of using the number "one" in the solution. This puzzle may be written on paper, instead of using matches.

Division by Subtraction

Say that you will use clock figures this time and that you will divide them to show that half of nine is four, half of eleven is six, and that half of twelve is seven.

Arrange the matches as shown above. Divide them by taking away the lower halves.

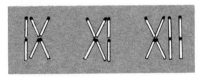

SUBTRACTION GAME FOR TWO PLAYERS

Place fifteen or nineteen matches near each other. You and the other player are to take turns removing

5

matches. One, two, or three matches can be taken at a time. The loser is the player who is left with the last match to take.

To win, you start by taking away two matches. Whatever the other player takes, you take what when added to his will make four. If he takes one, you take three. If he takes two, you take two. If he takes three, you take one. By playing this way you will always leave the last match for him.

If he wants to start the game but does not know the secret way of winning, try on your next to last turn to leave five matches. No matter what he then takes, you can always leave him the last match.

You can play this game with checkers, pebbles, wads of paper, or other small things.

ARITHMETIC AND SPELLING

Have eleven matches on the table and say to your friends, "You may not believe me, but I will add one to two to make one. I will do it by spelling." Position ten matches as shown, and count each match as you put it down. Say "Ten make TWO."

Ten Matches

Separate the ten matches that spell TWO. With an added eleventh match, spell ONE, as shown above.

Eleven Matches

DOWN TO UP

How to make a ground opening go up by taking away five matches.

Thirteen Matches

Eight Matches

A LITTLE TO A LOT

How to show it takes a lot to make a little and a little to make a lot.

Sixteen Matches

Eleven Matches

SMALLER IS BIGGER

How to prove a smaller word is bigger than a larger one by one match.

Twenty-Two Matches

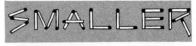

Twenty-One Matches

WEIGHTS AND MEASURES

How to show that there are more matches to an ounce than there are to a ton.

Twenty-Three Matches

Twelve Matches

How to show that half pints take more matches than quarts.

Twenty-Three Matches

Twenty Matches

How to show that there are more matches in a foot than in a mile.

Thirteen Matches

Eleven Matches

Do not tell your friends that the words are going to be spelled. Say that you will use matches to prove that big is small and small is big.

Make up your own words, such as: *sardine* and *eel, flower* and *tree,* or *mouse* and *cat.*

WALKING MATCHES

Take two matches and make a small slit in the end of one and pare the end of the other to make a small wedge.

Put the wedge into the slit as shown.

Place the matches over the sharp edge of a knife and hold the knife so that the match heads will touch on a table that has no cloth.

Hold the knife so that your hand will not rest on the table. You will find that you will not be able to keep the matches from walking or running along the table and sometimes falling off the end of the knife. You may use a hairpin instead of matches.

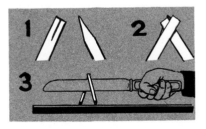

Sugar Tricks

IF YOU are at a party table where there is a bowl of lump sugar, you can have a lot of fun with your friends by doing sugar magic tricks for them. Do not announce that you want to do tricks, but have a secret helper tell somebody seated nearby that you can do some wonderful magic with sugar.

This helper, who may be your den chief, Den Mother, or another Cub Scout, could ask or have some other person ask you to do a couple of tricks.

You are to pretend that you are surprised and say something like, "Well, if you really want me to do a trick or two, I'll be glad to try."

Do not be in a hurry to say this. You want your audience to think that you are completely unprepared.

If a trick has to be prepared ahead of time, do the trick only once. You may be asked to do it again. Say that you have other tricks you want to do first, or that you have the magic power to do this trick only once in a while.

If you are with two or three friends and sugar is available, you need not wait for someone to ask you to perform. Just say that you know some sugar tricks that you would like to show them.

FEELING SUGAR WAVES

Tell your friends that sometimes you can feel waves, like electric waves, coming from lumps of sugar even when the lumps are covered. Say that you will leave the table and while you are gone somebody is to take a few lumps and cover them. Say, also, that when you come back you will feel the waves and tell how many lumps are covered.

A secret helper now takes over, having seen that he or she has the sugar bowl close at hand. Eight lumps are to be used. Nobody is to add a lump or take one away. Your helper is to see that neither happens.

A cup and a saucer are to be used as covers. Your helper may ask how many lumps are to go under the cup and how many under the saucer, or just count and cover them.

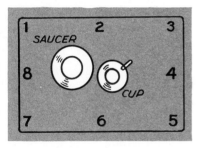

You and your helper are to plan and remember eight places around the table. Start at any corner as No. 1 and then as clock numbers go, follow with the other numbers. The picture shows such a plan.

The handle of the cup will let you know how many lumps are under the cup. Suppose your helper puts three there. When he puts the cup over them he points the handle to where you agreed the No. 3 place would be.

When you come back you see the handle but at once give all attention to the saucer under which you know there must be five lumps. Put a fin-

ger on the saucer and slowly say "one." Wait a moment and then say "two." Stop at "five." You are not supposed to know there are eight lumps being used. Put your fingers on the cup and count to three.

If paper cups and plates are used, your helper will have to put a nick or dent in the bottom edge of the cup or squeeze a small point on it. This mark can be used instead of a cup handle.

LUMP SUGAR SLAMMED FROM ITS PAPER WRAPPER AND THROUGH YOUR HAND

Secretly prepare for this trick by carefully taking the wrapper off the sugar so that there will not be the smallest tear in it. First open it at each end. Take the sugar out of the wrapper and fold the paper again so that it looks exactly the same as it did when the sugar was in it. You may have to have your den chief or Den Mother do this for you. If you practice a few times, you may be able to do it yourself, even at the table while people are busy talking. Prepare the sugar while holding it on your lap and, if you can, without looking at what you are doing.

If the trick is prepared away from the table, put the sugar back in its wrapper and then in a trouser pocket. At the table put the sugar on your lap and refold the wrapper. Hide the wrapper in your right hand.

Press the sugar into your left palm. Grip it by squeezing in the sides of your hand, as shown. You may bend fingers a little but not down on the

9

sugar. Put both hands on the table but do not look at them. Wait a few minutes. Be the last to reach into the sugar bowl.

WITH A LITTLE PRACTICE IT IS EASY TO HOLD THE SUGAR THIS WAY EVEN WITH YOUR PALM TURNED DOWN.

If nobody is looking, put the empty wrapper in the bowl and leave it there for a minute or so. If someone is looking, pretend that you are taking a lump. Either way, take the wrapper by its ends and hold it on top of the back of the hand holding the sugar. Now say, "Watch everybody."

← WRAPPER

SUGAR HELD IN YOUR PALM

Then say that "This is the magic way to get a lump of sugar out of its wrapper." Quickly raise your right hand and slam it down hard on the wrapper. At the same instant let the lump drop onto a plate, into a cup, or onto the table. The wrapper of

course will be flattened completely.

Practice gripping the sugar with a flat hand.

TELLING THE TURN AND SPELLING THE TURNER

Place eight lumps of sugar in a row on the table. Between each of them leave a space about the width of one lump, as shown here.

You and a secret helper are to think of the lumps as being numbered, the first being to your *left* when you are at the table. Your helper should be near the sugar. Say that you will leave the room and that while you are gone somebody is to turn a lump over and put it back in the row. When you are called in you will point out the lump that was turned and also the person who turned it. Your helper will keep his closed hands on the table, palms down.

When a sugar lump is turned, your helper is to slide out a finger to let you know the number of the lump. One finger means the first lump and all fingers the eighth. The numbering fingers are to be slightly bent.

When you come in, look at different people, among them your helper. You will have seen your helper's fingers. Pick up the lump that the fingers indicated and say, "This one."

Your helper now lets you know who did the turning. Left hand for a person to the helper's left and right for a person to the right. One

finger for a person next to the helper, two for the second person, and so on.

The person who turned will be near the sugar, which means not far from your helper.

If the person is across the table, your helper is to put a left or right arm on the table to let you know whether the person is to your left or right. Fingers will give the person's number. One closed hand for a person alone at the left end. No hands for a person alone at the right.

Say you have to spell *sugar* to find out who did the turning. Spell *S-U-G-A-R* twice, pointing at some person each time you say a letter. Spell slowly the second time. Begin to spell a third time. When you have said "S" and pointed, wait a second and then suddenly point at the turner and say "U" as loud as you can.

CROSSED LINES

Let your friends see you put a mark on your palm with burnt match charcoal or a fountain pen and another mark of the same length on a lump of sugar. Say that the mark on your hand can sometimes act like a magnet and get the mark off the sugar. The sugar is dropped into a glass of water and your hand with the mark on it is put on top of the glass. When the sugar has melted a little, take your hand off the glass and show it. Where there was one

mark on your hand there will now be another mark across it.

Make a slanting mark across the line on your hand as shown. Close your hand but keep your fingers as straight as you can and pointing to your wrist. Squeeze hard where the mark is.

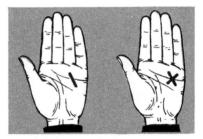

When you open your hand you should find an X crossing the line.

Doing the Trick

You may squeeze your hand to get the X when you are marking the sugar or when dropping the lump into the glass. Say that people do not always see the mark coming up through the water to your hand. If you drop the sugar into soda water, tell your friends to look for bits of the mark coming up with the bubbles.

Double-Crossing

You may follow up on the trick if you get a chance to make an X on your thumb without being seen. Make it with your hands on your lap. When ready, ask a friend to

11

make an X on a lump and drop the sugar in the glass. Say "I want you to hold your hand on the glass, like this." Take his hand with your fingers on top and press your thumb against his palm as you bring his hand over to put it on the glass. He will already have the X on his hand. Tell him to wait a few seconds before he takes his hand off the glass.

Not using sugar, make a mark on the back as well as the front of your hand. Rub the back one off and show that it went through your hand to make an X.

SUGAR THROUGH A HANDKERCHIEF

You will need a small rubber band that may have to be doubled if it is not small enough.

Secretly put a small rubber band around your right thumb and two or three fingers, and then hold a lump of sugar as shown. Put a handkerchief over this hand and bring both hands up from your lap. With left hand spread the handkerchief on the table. The covered right hand is now to put its sugar down quietly.

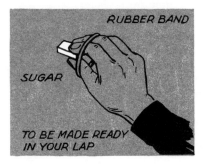

Keep the rubber band on thumb and fingers by spreading them a little bit.

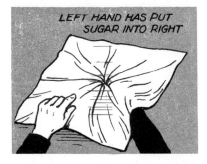

With left hand take a lump from the sugar bowl and place it so that the right thumb and fingers can grip it with the handkerchief. Say that you are going to push the sugar all the way through. Push it well down. The right hand is now to let the rubber band slip off. The band will go over the sugar and make a tight little bag to hold it. Take the right hand out from under the handkerchief. There are now two hidden lumps, one on the table.

Both hands are now free. With your right take up the handkerchief at its center and lift off to show the sugar on table.

With both hands take the handkerchief, keeping the bag on your side, and shake gently a few times. Pocket the handkerchief.

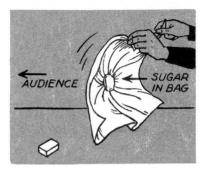

FUNNY COUNTING

Put four sugar lumps in a row on the table and ask your friends "How much is three times four?" "Twelve" you will be told.

Pick up a lump, put it down, and say "one." Pick up and put down as you count along the row three times until you reach "twelve."

Say "All right, but three times four does not always come to twelve. I will again count three times."

Here you see how to do the second counting to get eleven.

The trick comes when you have counted to eight. This time you do not start at the left end of the row, but you put number eight down, pick up the lump next to it, put it down as nine and the other two as ten and eleven. The drawing shows how.

If you are asked to do this counting again, you can do it differently. When you come to four, put it down. Count the next one as five and the other two as six and seven. Then count either from right or left —eight, nine, ten, eleven.

Now say that three times four does not always make eleven either.

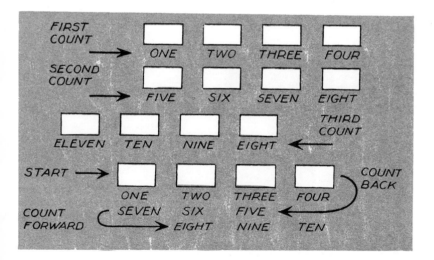

This time you fake at each end of the row and, starting at the left end, count as shown by the arrows.

The counting must be rapid and without stops.

MORE FUNNY COUNTING

This time four times three makes ten. As you do this trick ask your friends to watch carefully. Then ask others to do it. When they have tried and failed, do it once more and then let them try again.

You must be neither too slow nor too fast with this counting.

Have three sugar lumps on the table. With one hand pick up a lump and put it into your other hand, counting "one." Pick up another lump, put it with the first, and count "two." Pick up the third lump, put it with the others, and count "three." Now take them one at a time from your hand and count "four, five, six" as you put them on the table.

Pick them up again, one at a time,

and count "seven, eight." Stop a moment and move aside the lump that you would have counted as "nine" if you had picked it up. One at a time, take the two from your hand and, as you put them down, say "nine, ten."

Now for the puzzle part. Take up the three lumps and put them into some person's hand. Point toward the table and ask this person to count as you did. He will not be able to do the trick. Neither will anybody to whom you give the sugar.

Here Is the Secret

When you do the trick you PICK UP the lumps as you count. The person you give them to starts counting as the lumps are PUT DOWN. He takes the lumps from the hand where you put them when you ask him to start counting.

TEN-LUMP PLACING

With ten lumps of sugar on the table ask your friends to put them in five rows so that there will be four lumps in each row. Let them try for a while.

Do not be in a hurry to show how the lumps are to be placed.

Your friends will find this to be a real puzzle.

The picture shows you how to get the five rows each having four lumps.

If one of your friends knows the secret he will, if he is a good Cub Scout, also be a good sport and will not show how the lumps are to be

GIVE THE SUGAR TO GET THE COUNTING STARTED.

POINT AT THE TABLE.

placed, nor will he tell anyone that he knows how. He will let you show how the puzzle is done.

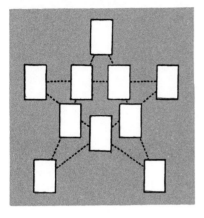

NINE-LUMP PLACING

When you have shown how the ten-lump puzzle is done, remove a lump and ask to have nine lumps placed to make ten rows with three lumps to a row. Again, give your friends time to try to do this puzzle. The picture shows how.

This trick and some of the count-

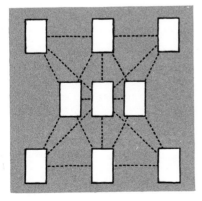

ing ones can be done with checkers, pebbles, bottle caps, or wads of paper when you are not at a table where you can get lumps of sugar.

SUGAR-LUMP CATCHING

Hold a small paper cup as shown, and between finger and thumb put one lump with another on top of it. Toss up the top lump and catch it in the cup. To get the second lump in, do not toss it. Let go of it and quickly put the cup under it. Ask your friends to try before you show how. To catch the second needs lots of practice.

TO CATCH THE SECOND NEEDS LOTS OF PRACTICE.

LUMP JUMPING

Place ten lumps of sugar in a row and ask any person at the table to take a lump, jump it over two on either side, and put it on the third lump away from it to make a pair.

This is to be done with five lumps until there are five pairs. Only two lumps, either single or as a pair, are to be jumped over at a time.

For practicing, mark numbers on the lumps, but learn to do the trick

1 2 3 4 5 6 7 8 9 10

without marking them. First jump 4 over 2 and 3 to make a pair with 1. Next pair 6 with 9 over 7 and 8. There will be open spaces, so 8 crosses them, jumping 7 and 5 to pair with 3. Jumping this pair, 2 pairs with 5. This leaves 10 to jump 6 and 9 and pair with 7.

TURNING THE DOTS

Mark a dot on each one of the ten lumps and arrange them as shown. Ask anybody to start from any lump, skip two, and turn the next one over.

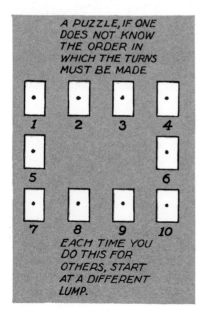

A PUZZLE, IF ONE DOES NOT KNOW THE ORDER IN WHICH THE TURNS MUST BE MADE

1 2 3 4

5 6

7 8 9 10

EACH TIME YOU DO THIS FOR OTHERS, START AT A DIFFERENT LUMP.

Suppose the start is at 3. Going left, 2 and 1 are to be skipped and 5 turned. If to the right, 4 and 6 are skipped to turn 10. Each start is to be from a lump with the dot side up, but the skip count may be on any lump. The puzzle is to turn down all dots except one.

The secret: The lump you count from each time is the next to be turned over.

WHO ATE THE LUMP?

Leave the room. While you are gone, have someone eat a lump of sugar on the table near your helper. When you return, all hands are flat on the table. Walk around, touch a few cheeks and fingers. Say, "Not you" until you come to the person who ate the lump. Your helper will let you know who as he did for the other tricks.

A JOKE VANISH

Place a cup over a lump of sugar and say that you will not touch the cup but will make the sugar beneath vanish. Move a hand over the cup and say, "That's all." Wait until your helper or another person lifts the cup. Take the lump, put it in your mouth, and chew it.

Say, "It's gone and I didn't touch the cup."

Checker Tricks,
Puzzles, and Games

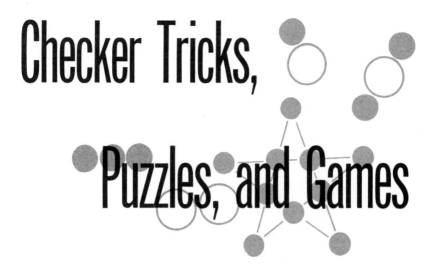

WHILE YOU are doing your magic with checkers, someone may ask you to repeat certain tricks. Say that you have more to do and that you may want help with some of them. Do not repeat the trick, and DO NOT show how it was done. However, a lot of the following tricks may be done over and over again, giving your friends a chance to see how the moves are made, but still keeping them puzzled.

For a number of these tricks you may use coins instead of checkers. You may even use pop-bottle caps of different colors, or if you are outdoors, some of the games may be played with pebbles. For some games you will need cardboard or paper with certain marked lines or spaces. Outdoors, some of these markings may be scraped on the ground with a stick.

To learn some of these tricks and games with checkers or coins, it is best to cut out cardboard disks and mark them A, B, C, D, and so on, so that you can follow the moves shown here in the pictures.

RING THE CHANGE

Use six checkers of the same color, or six coins all the same, in two rows. The puzzle is to move only three of the six, one at a time, and put them with the other three so as to have all six in a circle.

When the two rows are first set up, ask friends to do the trick, and when they have failed, which most likely they will, you make the moves quickly so that they will not have time to catch on.

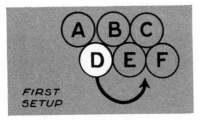

FIRST SETUP

Move D to touch both E and F.

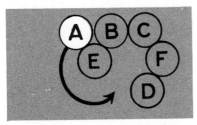

Move E to touch both A and B.

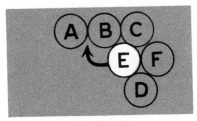

A over D and E.

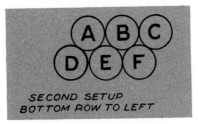

SECOND SETUP
BOTTOM ROW TO LEFT

A to touch E and D.

Set checkers or coins up again as in Fig. 4 and ask your friends to try once more. Some person might notice the difference in the setup and ask you to do it again. You can do it by making the moves in reverse. Move F under D and E. Move E to touch B and C. Bring C around to touch E and F.

You can also do the first setup a different way as if it were upside down. Move C to touch A and B. Move B to touch E and F. Move F to touch B and C.

MOVING COLORS

Put six checkers, three red and three black, in a row, each red checker followed by a black one as shown. If you use coins, follow dimes with pennies.

Only three moves are to be made and only two checkers are to be moved at the same time. When the three moves have been made, the row of checkers should be three blacks followed by three reds.

Making the moves, use two fingers of one hand or a finger and thumb. Before doing this puzzle, ask your friends to try. Give them lots of time before you show them how to do it.

Move B and C to the left of A.

Move E and F to where B and C were.

Move F and D to the left of B.

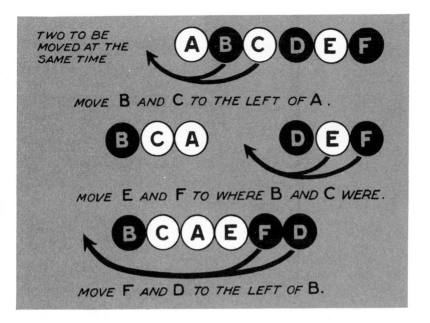

TWO TO BE
MOVED AT THE
SAME TIME

MOVE B AND C TO THE LEFT OF A.

MOVE E AND F TO WHERE B AND C WERE.

MOVE F AND D TO THE LEFT OF B.

ONE DOUBLE MOVE AND ALL CHANGE

Sixteen checkers or sixteen coins are arranged in a square of four rows, each row down having four checkers of the same color, or if coins, the same kind of coin. If the front row is red checkers, then the second row has to be black, the third row red, and the fourth black.

If using coins, the first row may be dimes, the second row pennies, the third dimes, and fourth pennies.

The checkers or coins in the rows of four across all touch each other, but there should be a little space between each of the four rows as shown in the drawing.

Only one move is to be made. Two checkers or coins are to be

moved at the same time with two fingers of the same hand or with finger and thumb.

When the move has been made and the two checkers or coins are back in the square, all of the rows

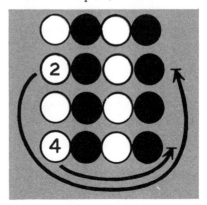

19

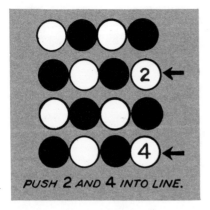

PUSH 2 AND 4 INTO LINE.

should be of alternating colors, as shown in the second drawing. Use a smooth surface for the moving.

Move the second and fourth in the first down row to the other end of their rows across.

With the second and fourth, push their rows across to the right and the down rows will be changed.

TRIANGLE TURNABOUT

Place ten checkers of the same color or ten coins of the same kind on a smooth flat surface and arrange them so that they make a triangle pointing away from you. Do not put the checkers or coins too close to each other.

Say that the ten are airplanes or, better yet, flying saucers, leaving their home base. To get back home only three of the saucers are to fly out in straight lines to make a new triangle to point in your direction. None of the three is to be lifted, but moved only in straight lines. Do not be in a hurry to show how, but give

your friends lots of time to try the moves themselves.

Flight of saucers leaving their base in a triangle formation.

About to return. Lead saucer flies to the right of the two that were behind it.

Slide the left saucer of the bottom row forward to be in line with the top row.

Slide the saucer at the right of what was the bottom row to make it the leader.

If you want to have what was the first or lead saucer be the leading one returning you will have to repeat the moves twice. Use a coin different from the others or a different-colored checker as the leader.

Start with the first turnabout pictured. Move C to left in line with the two coins above it. Move A down to be in the line with C, and B to the top of the triangle.

Now move C to be the leader home. Move B to the right of the two under it. Move C up to complete the rear line of four.

THE START

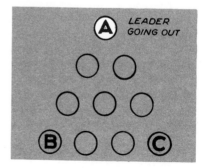

LEADER GOING OUT

To know A, B, and C when practicing, stick bits of marked paper on them.

FIRST MOVE

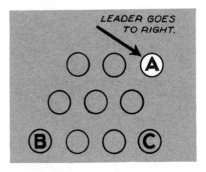

SECOND MOVE

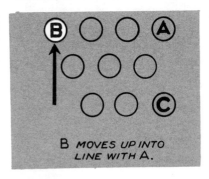

LAST MOVE

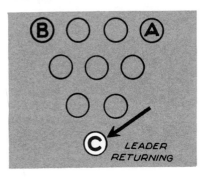

THREE IN A ROW

On a piece of paper or cardboard draw a design as shown below. Your drawing ought to be about eight inches wide and four and a half deep. Mark points in the center of the lines on each side and top and bottom. Finish by drawing lines from corner to corner through the point where the other lines cross each other in the center of the design. There will be nine points where the lines join, but do not mark them with letters the way they are shown here. These letters are to help you learn the game and to show you how to win.

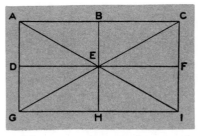

There are to be two players, each having three checkers. One player has red and the other black. The first player puts a checker on one of the points, then the second player puts down one of his, and so on, in turn, until all six checkers are down. If a player is able to put his three checkers in a straight line, he has won the game.

If, when all six have been put down, neither player has his in line, the moving begins. The one who puts the first checker down has the first move. This move is not to be more than sliding a checker from one point to the next point, such as from G to H, D, or E; H to G, I, or E; and from the center point E to any of the other uncovered points.

Arrange by "heads or tails" on coins, or any other way you like, who is to begin the game. The best point on which to put the first checker is E in the center.

If you have the center and the other player has put his checker down, the best way to be almost sure of winning is to put your next checker down two points away from his. If he puts his at C, put yours at either A or I. If he puts his first checker at D or F, put your second at B or H.

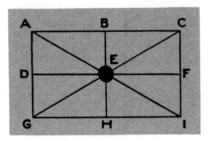

If he sees that you will get your three checkers in line by putting your third at I to win, he may put his second there to stop you. If he puts

his second on I, put your third on F to stop him. All you have to do then, since you have the first move, is to slide your checker down from A to D to win the game.

Suppose the other player has center and you put your first at C and he puts his second at B, put your second at H. If he puts his second at I, put your second at A. If he puts his at D, put yours at F. The reason you do this is to stop him from putting his checkers down in line.

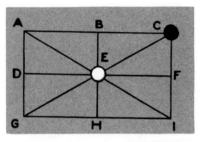

Sometimes, in making the moves, a checker may be forced out of the center. This drawing shows where the checker at A can move only to B or the center one will have to move out. If checker at A moves to B, move yours at D up to A. The center one must now move out. Move in from C.

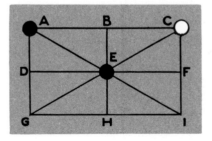

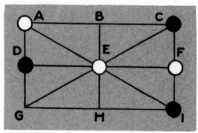

THE EIGHT-POINTER PUZZLE

On paper or cardboard draw the eight-pointer as shown here. Use a ruler and draw the lines *A-B* and *C-D* two inches away from each other. Make the lines six inches long. Make the lines *E-F* and *G-H* the same length and the same distance from each other. Next draw the lines from *A* to *H*, from *E* to *D*, from *G* to *C*, and from *B* to *F*. Put the letters on your drawing for practice only. Make a new drawing when you are ready to puzzle your friends.

Use seven checkers or coins for this puzzle. What you have to do is to put a checker or coin, or even a little rolled wad of paper, on one of the points, slide it along to the other end of a line, and leave it there.

Next, put down another checker or whatever you are using on another point and slide it along a line to the point at the other end. Keep doing this until all seven are on points. You are not to start from a point already covered.

All you have to do to get the seven checkers on points is to remember that after you have moved your checker from one point along a line to another point, the next point to be covered is the one from which you have just moved.

As there are two lines going to each point, you can change your moves each time when asked to do it again by someone who wants to find out how you make the moves. Practice first by moving along a line to cover the point at the end. Any point will do as a start. Next, start at the end of a line that leads to the point from where you began the puzzle.

For example, suppose you began at point *F* and moved your checker

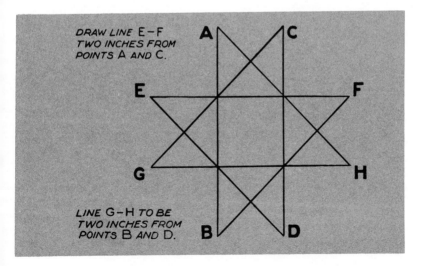

DRAW LINE E-F TWO INCHES FROM POINTS A AND C.

LINE G-H TO BE TWO INCHES FROM POINTS B AND D.

or coin to cover E. The next move is from B to cover F. Then from A to cover B, followed by H to A, G to H, C to G, and lastly, from D to cover C.

To make it harder for your friends to follow and remember your moves as you repeat the puzzle, each time start from a different point for the first move. You will notice that when you have two points covered, as when you moved from F to cover E and from B to cover F, you have two vacant starting points, each leading to a covered point. You can continue as before, by covering B from A, or you may choose covering D by moving down from C. If you make this latter move, the next move to be made is from G to cover point C. Then cover H by moving from A. Now you will have an open line from A to B, and you take your choice as to whether you move from A to B or from B to A.

"MUST NOT" MOVING

On a smooth surface place in a row and touching each other three coins of the same size. You are NOT to TOUCH A or MOVE B. The puzzle is to get C between A and B.

With left-hand finger keep B from moving, and with right-hand finger slide C to the right. Now

slam C against B. A will shoot off to the right. Slide C around to the left of B.

A and B may be pennies and C may be a dime.

SQUARE PLAY

On cardboard or paper draw an eight-inch or a twelve-inch square and divide it into sixteen small squares as shown. There are to be two players, one of them with four red checkers and the other with four black. Four dimes and four pennies will do instead. The players agree on who is to put the first checker or coin on one of the small squares. The second player then puts his checker down on another square. The players are to take turns until each has his four checkers placed in four squares.

To win the game a player must get his four checkers in a row either up and down, across, or diagonally as shown from A to D or from C to D. If a player is able to put his checkers down in a row right at the start, he has already won the game. Watch to see if your opponent has three in a row. Put one of yours where he could put his fourth. If neither set of four is placed in a row, the moves begin. The moves can be made in any direction, but only to the next square.

There is no jumping one checker over another in this game. A smart player may win in a few moves. If players are evenly matched the game may go on for a long, long time.

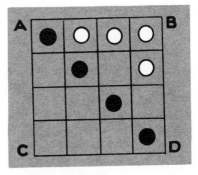

Where black wins.

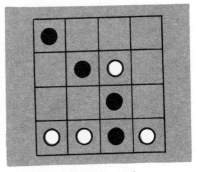

Moves have to be made.

CAN YOU DO?

Take ten checkers or coins and ask your friends if they can put the ten or some portion of them in a certain number of straight rows with a certain number in each row, as described below. When they have tried and failed, as most of them likely will, you show them how.

The drawings show how to place the checkers or the coins.

How to place ten in five rows with four in each row. Were you asked to do this you would not find it easy if you had not seen the picture below.

How to put seven in four rows with three in each row is shown.

With six coins, arrange two rows, having four in each row.

Put the bottom one on top of the one in the center.

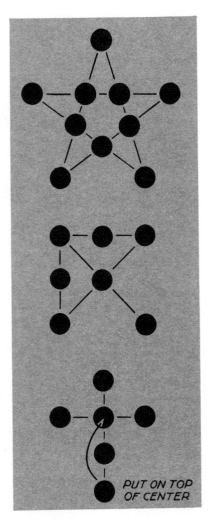

PUT ON TOP OF CENTER

25

THE SAME COLORS TOGETHER IN FOUR MOVES

Use four red and four black checkers. All eight are to be put in a row and no two of the same color are to be side by side.

The puzzle is to move two checkers or coins at a time and in four moves get four of one color at one end of the row and four of the other color at the other end.

To help you learn the moves, numbers are given here. Stick bits of paper on your checkers or coins and have them numbered as shown.

Reverse these moves if you want to get the row the way it was at the start.

This puzzle may be done with wads of paper, bottle caps, or pebbles if you can get two sets of four, each set of a different color.

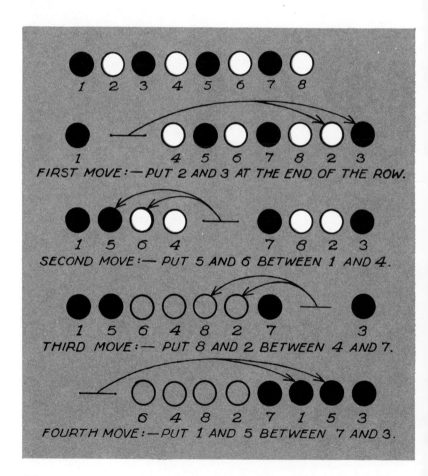

1 2 3 4 5 6 7 8

FIRST MOVE:— PUT 2 AND 3 AT THE END OF THE ROW.

SECOND MOVE:— PUT 5 AND 6 BETWEEN 1 AND 4.

THIRD MOVE:— PUT 8 AND 2 BETWEEN 4 AND 7.

FOURTH MOVE:—PUT 1 AND 5 BETWEEN 7 AND 3.

CHECKER JUMPING PUZZLE

Draw twenty-five squares and put nine checkers on the center squares as shown. All checkers except the one on the exact center square are to be of the same color. You can jump any checker over the one next to it where there is an empty square at the other side. The jump can be made in any direction and more than one jump can be made if there are empty squares. A jumped checker is to be taken off the board as in a regular checker game. To finish the puzzle, all of the same-colored checkers must be taken off by the jumping and the odd-colored one jumped back into the center square. To help you practice, the checkers are numbered here and the moves shown by arrows.

When you have learned the moves, practice looking at the pictures turned sideways or upside down so that you will be able to do the puzzle seemingly different ways.

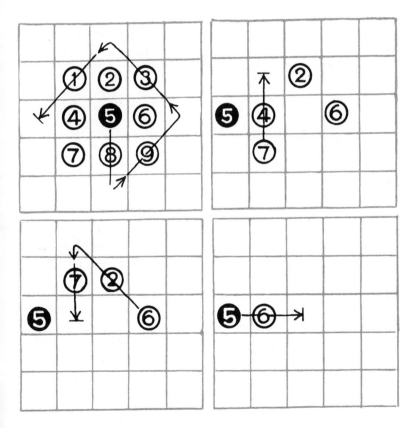

MORE MOVES

Arrange two red checkers and three black ones in a row as shown. If using coins—two nickels followed by three pennies. To help you practice, letter bits of paper and stick to the checkers or coins as shown below.

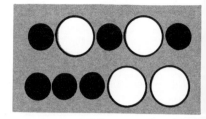

The puzzle is to move two side-by-side checkers at the same time and in five moves to get the checkers positioned as shown at right.

Ask your friends to try first and

give them time before you show them how. Count each move as you make it.

Next show that you can do the puzzle in four moves.

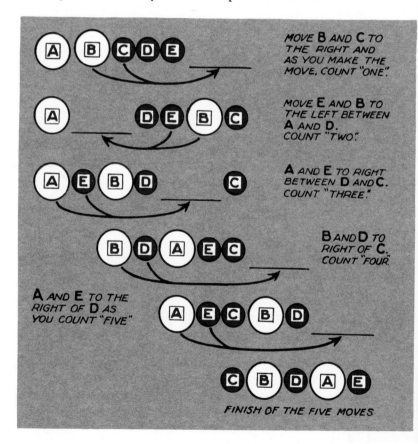

MOVE **B** AND **C** TO THE RIGHT AND AS YOU MAKE THE MOVE, COUNT "ONE".

MOVE **E** AND **B** TO THE LEFT BETWEEN **A** AND **D**. COUNT "TWO".

A AND **E** TO RIGHT BETWEEN **D** AND **C**. COUNT "THREE".

B AND **D** TO RIGHT OF **C**. COUNT "FOUR".

A AND **E** TO THE RIGHT OF **D** AS YOU COUNT "FIVE"

FINISH OF THE FIVE MOVES

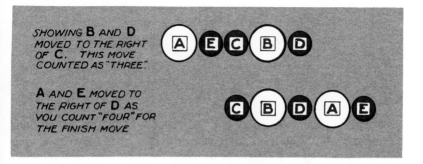

SHOWING B AND D MOVED TO THE RIGHT OF C. THIS MOVE COUNTED AS "THREE."

A AND E MOVED TO THE RIGHT OF D AS YOU COUNT "FOUR" FOR THE FINISH MOVE

To do the same trick in four moves, the first two moves are the same as when doing the trick in five moves. The third and fourth moves are shown above.

Move B and D to the right of C. Count "three."

Move A and B to the right of D. Count "four."

Do these five and four moves over and over again with the checkers or coins with the lettered papers attached. Then try over and over again without the letters and without looking at the pictures on these pages. Do not do these tricks for anybody until you are sure you can make all the moves quickly.

PICKUP—LAST MAN LOSES

Put twenty-one checkers in three rows so as to have seven checkers in each row. Two players are to take turns in picking up and removing the checkers. A player may take one, two, or three checkers at a time, but not more than three. The player who finds that the last checker is left for him, loses the game.

How to win: Let the other player start first. No matter what number he takes, you just take a number which if added to what he took will make four. If he takes three you take one. If he takes two you take two. By doing this the last one will always be left for him.

After losing a few games, he may ask you to start first. If this happens you will have to play so that in your next to last pickup there will be five left in the last row. Then if he takes three you take one. If he takes two you take two, if he takes three you take one, and he loses again.

Set the rows up again and tell your friend that he can take as many as four. Whatever he takes, you pick up what if added to his will make five. If he takes three, you take two, and so on until the last one is left for him.

Like the other games, the pickup can be played with bottle caps, pebbles, small wads of paper, coins, sticks or matches. These checker puzzlers and games will be helpful to entertain your friends and to keep the den busy during the den meeting.

Money Magic

IT IS NOT easy to keep real coins to use just for doing magic tricks. Imitation coins that you can get at toy counters in dime stores or at trick and puzzle stores, if you live in a big city, will do just as well.

A trick must seem like magic and you must pretend that it is, so do not tell anybody how it is done. When you have a coin in your hand that you do not want anybody to know about, do not look at your hand. You may point with it, but look the way you are pointing. Be careful to hold the coin so that it will not slip from your hand and spoil your act.

For some of the coin tricks you will need cloth napkins or handkerchiefs. They may be white or colored but without patterns.

If you can do things better with your left hand than with your right, reverse the instructions that are given here.

STACKING AND PLACING COINS

This is a trick where you stack seven coins of the same kind on top of each other and hold them between the thumb and fingers of one hand.

The other hand takes the top coin and places it on a table or flat surface. The second coin is then to be taken and put at the bottom of the stack. The third coin is put on the table beside the first, and the fourth put under the stack. The fifth coin, which is now at the top of the stack, is taken and put on the table in line with the two already there. The top coin is put under the stack. You will now be holding four coins between the fingers and thumb of one hand.

The top one of the four goes to the table and the next one under the stack. The top one of the three goes to the table and the next one goes under the last coin in the stack. The top one of the two goes to the table and the one left is now put down beside it. When they are all down, the coins should be in the order of "Heads - Tails - Heads - Tails - Heads - Tails - Heads." When putting the coins on the table, none are to be turned over.

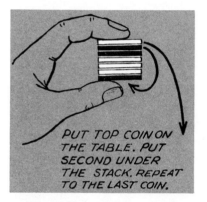

PUT TOP COIN ON THE TABLE. PUT SECOND UNDER THE STACK. REPEAT TO THE LAST COIN.

The secret is in the stacking. The first or top coin should be "heads," the next two "tails," next three "heads," and last, or bottom coin, "tails."

Be careful not to let any coins drop when you are doing this trick, and do not tell how you stacked them.

The coins should all be the same, but are shown here as white and black so that you can see how to stack them. The whites are "heads" and the black ones "tails."

BIG THROUGH LITTLE

You can make a quarter go through a dime-sized hole.

Put a dime on a piece of white paper and with a sharp pencil close to the dime draw around the coin so as to make a circle the size of the dime. Remove the dime and fold the paper in half across the circle. With sharp scissors cut the half circle so that when the paper is opened flat again, you will have a round hole the size of the dime.

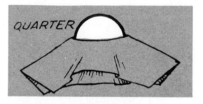

QUARTER

Push the dime through the hole and then put the quarter under the paper with a part of it coming up through the hole. Take hold of this part and with the free hand bend the paper down around the coin. This will make the hole into a long narrow slit through which you can pull the quarter up easily without tearing the paper.

FOR A SPIN

With the first finger of your left hand, hold a quarter crosswise and standing on its edge. Keep the other fingers and thumb bent in out of the way.

With the first finger of your right hand quickly stroke along and off the end of the finger holding the quarter, but do not press down too hard. At the fourth or fifth stroke secretly let the tip of your thumb hit the edge of the coin which should spin away free. Practice until you can make the coin spin every time.

COIN THROUGH HANDKERCHIEF

First finger and thumb hold up a half dollar to be seen by all. Other three fingers are closed.

Left hand spreads a handkerchief over the right so that the coin will be in the center.

One handkerchief corner should lie on your arm and the opposite corner hang down in front.

To show that the coin is still under the handkerchief lift up the front corner and bring it all the way over to the corner on the right arm. Right thumb must keep holding the little tuck.

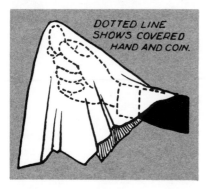

Now for the important part of the trick.

Left hand takes hold of the coin through handkerchief as if to fix it so that the round shape could be seen. While left hand holds the coin, the right thumb secretly makes a little tuck in the handkerchief and grips the tuck against the coin as shown.

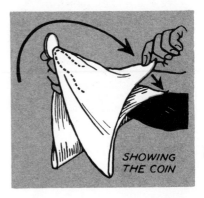

When coin has been shown the left hand lifts both of the corners of the sleeve and lets them droop down in front. It will look as if the coin has been covered again. It will be under but outside.

Left hand takes all of the hanging corners and gives a few twists.

Saying that you will make the

coin come through the handkerchief, slowly pull with the left hand, or

BOTH CORNERS TO HANG IN FRONT.

COIN IS NOW UNDER, BUT OUTSIDE.

LEFT HAND TAKES HANDKERCHIEF AWAY FROM THE RIGHT WHICH IS HOLDING THE COIN.

COIN SHAPE IS SEEN.

YOU MAY LET ANY PERSON PULL THE HANDKERCHIEF AWAY.

COIN COMES OUT FREE.

let a friend do the pulling, which must not be rough.

Right hand pulling in the opposite direction comes away holding the coin between the first finger and thumb.

With a little practice the two corners on the sleeve may be flipped over to hang down in front. Just swing the right hand out and down.

THE DISAPPEARING COIN

Hold up a coin between your left thumb and first finger and then cover it with a handkerchief. With the right thumb and first finger take the coin and handkerchief away from the left hand. Your right hand will be outside the handkerchief and holding the coin through it. Ask a friend to put his hand under the handkerchief and touch the coin, as shown.

Ask several people to touch the coin in the same way to make sure that it is there. Now for the magic!

You have a secret helper. He is to be the LAST person to touch the coin.

He acts like the others who touched the coin but, under cover of the handkerchief, he closes his hand around the coin and takes it away from you. He may say "O.K." or, "It's there all right." He should not be in a hurry to put the coin in his pocket, but should wait until you have everybody looking at what you are doing. He must not look at his hand, but like the others, he must keep looking at you.

With your left hand make a couple of circles over your right, which is holding the handkerchief, and say that you are making the magic sign that will cause the coin to disappear.

Suddenly throw the handkerchief in the air. Catch it with both hands and spread it out to show that the coin has gone! This is when your friend pockets the coin.

THE INVISIBLE FLYING COIN

This is another way to end the disappearing coin trick. While your friends are touching the coin under the handkerchief, it will be easy to secretly take another coin from your left trouser pocket with your left hand. Do not be in a hurry getting it, and do not hold it in a tight grip. Do not look at this hand, but look at the right hand or at the person touching the handkerchief coin.

When your secret helper has taken the coin this time, you do not make the magic sign with your left hand.

Stretch your right arm to the right, look at the handkerchief and say, "Now the magic sign." While you say this, bring your closed left hand up slowly, but do not stretch out your left arm.

To make the magic sign, swing the handkerchief in a few small circles. Then quickly snap the handkerchief half way over towards the left hand and say "There it goes!" For the first time look at your left hand. Open it, show coin and say, "Boy, did you see it go!"

SWING AROUND A FEW TIMES IN SMALL CIRCLES.

TOUCHED COIN COMES THROUGH HANDKERCHIEF

Have two coins in your right trouser pocket. Take both out at the same time, holding one between your first finger and thumb and the second coin, which must not be seen, covered by your other three fingers.

Show the first coin and with your left hand, cover coin and the right hand holding it with a handkerchief.

With your left hand take both coin and handkerchief away from the right hand.

Left hand covers and then takes handkerchief and coin from the right hand, shown at right.

LEFT HAND COVERS THE RIGHT AND THE COIN.

LEFT TAKES HOLD OF COIN.

Right hand points at the handkerchief. Ask people to touch the coin.

LEFT HAND TAKES HANDKERCHIEF AND COIN AWAY FROM THE RIGHT HAND.

SECOND COIN IS HIDDEN IN THE CLOSED RIGHT HAND.

Before anyone does this, take the handkerchief and coin from the left hand as shown on page 36. One coin will now be under the handkerchief and the other outside it hidden in your hand. When your secret helper touches and takes the coin, say that you are going to make it come through the handkerchief.

Take all four corners in your left hand. Move the right down a little bit to get a good grip on the handkerchief, but be careful not to drop the coin. When all set, yank your

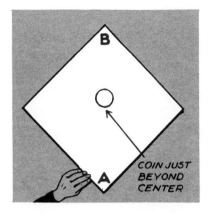

SECOND COIN STAYS HIDDEN IN THE RIGHT HAND.

RIGHT HAND TAKES THE COVERED COIN BACK FROM LEFT.

COIN JUST BEYOND CENTER

right hand away and show the coin that had been hidden in it.

Important—Do not yank too hard. You might drop and lose coin.

Place a coin on a napkin that is on a table. Corner *A* is to be near the table edge near you.

LEFT HAND TAKES HOLD OF THE CORNERS.

RIGHT HAND WITH COIN, TO YANK AWAY FROM THE HANDKERCHIEF AND SHOW COIN.

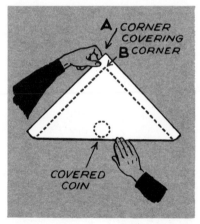

A CORNER COVERING B CORNER

COVERED COIN

COIN THROUGH HANDKERCHIEF OR NAPKIN ON TABLE

For this trick there should be a cloth on the table so that when the coin drops the sound will not be heard. The handkerchief or napkin used should NOT be the thin sort that can be seen through.

Take corner *A* and fold the handkerchief away from you, bringing *A* over and about an inch beyond the corner *B*. The coin is now covered.

With both hands take hold of the coin through the handkerchief or napkin and roll both of them away from you.

When the roll is almost over to

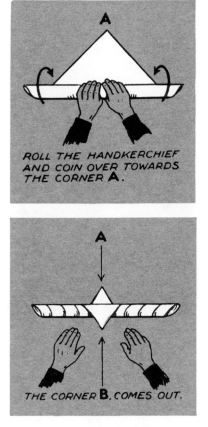

ROLL THE HANDKERCHIEF AND COIN OVER TOWARDS THE CORNER A.

THE CORNER B, COMES OUT.

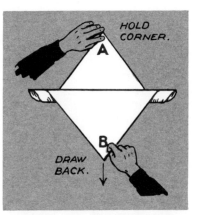

HOLD CORNER.

A

B

DRAW BACK.

A   COIN HAS VANISHED.

B

corner *A,* the corner *B* will come out on your side. Stop rolling, because *B* must not go over corner *A.*

Put a finger of one hand on corner *A* to hold it down. With thumb and finger of the other hand take corner *B* and draw it back slowly to your side of the table.

The coin has disappeared. It will be under the handkerchief. Pick this up, show the coin, and say that it was magic that made it go through.

COIN THROUGH THREE NAPKINS—AND—

This time you do not need a table-cloth because you want your audience to hear the coin each time that you put it down on the napkins. Except for the last move, all moves are the same as in "coin through the handkerchief or napkin." You may use paper napkins.

Stack three napkins on the table with their corners in the same position as were the corners of the handkerchief. Place the coin on top a little beyond the center the same way as you did for the single handkerchief or napkin trick. When putting the coin down tap or snap it so that the sound will be heard.

Say that you are going to make the coin pass through the top napkin onto the second. Do this the same way as you did with the single handkerchief.

Lift top napkin and show the coin on the second. Replace the napkin and put the coin on top of it again. Say that you are going to pass the coin through two napkins this time. Tap the coin on the napkins.

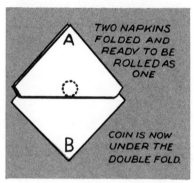

Use the top and second napkins as if they were one napkin. Take up the two *A* corners together and put them over and a little bit beyond the *B* corners.

Roll up the same way as before until the *B* corners come out to be pulled back. The coin will be on the third napkin.

Now say that you will pass the coin through three napkins. Again take up the coin and put it once more on top of the three stacked napkins, giving the coin a good tap as you put it down.

Some of your audience may think they know how you pass the coin, but they are in for a big surprise.

This time after showing the coin,

get most of it into your hand as you tap it. Have the three *A* corners ready to lift before you tap. The tap and lift should be done almost at the same time.

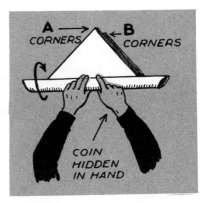

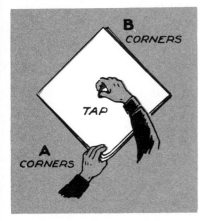

Bring back all of the three corners together. Then take up the napkins one at a time.

The moment you tap, bring the *A* corners over towards *B* corners covering the hand holding the coin. This hand steals the coin and is ready to help the other hand roll the napkins up over the *B* corners.

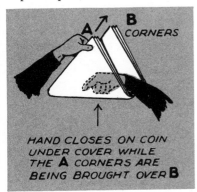

Three fingers of the right hand hold the coin as the finger and thumb help other hand roll.

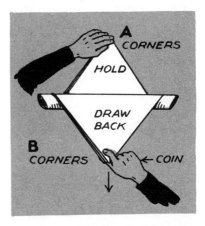

With your free hand pick up the top napkin by one of its corners and, with the other hand holding the hidden coin, point at the second napkin and say "Well, it went through the first napkin."

With the same hand that holds the coin, pick up the second napkin and say, "It went through this one too—and—"

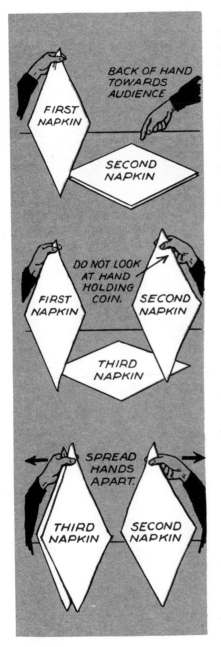

BACK OF HAND
TOWARDS
AUDIENCE

FIRST
NAPKIN

SECOND
NAPKIN

DO NOT LOOK
AT HAND
HOLDING
COIN.

FIRST
NAPKIN

SECOND
NAPKIN

THIRD
NAPKIN

SPREAD
HANDS
APART.

THIRD
NAPKIN

SECOND
NAPKIN

Pick up the third napkin with the hand that picked up the first one so that it will be holding two napkins. As you are about to pick up this napkin say, "It went through this one."

Now for your act! There will be nothing on the table when the last napkin is lifted, and you must look very surprised. Look up and down along the table and shake the napkins. Say that the coin must have gone through the table. The hand with two napkins goes on top of the table, the other, with napkin and coin, underneath. Tap with both hands and bring out the coin.

A much more magic way to end the napkin trick needs more practice, but it is not very hard to do. For this trick, the heavier the napkin paper the better. Cloth napkins instead of paper ones may be used.

When you take up the first napkin hold it up high enough to cover your left breast pocket, the flap of which should be open. Taking up the second napkin with the hand holding the coin, bring it behind the first and let the coin drop into the pocket. Immediately leave this second napkin with the first and bring down the hand that held the coin to point at and pick up the third napkin. As you pick this third one up, put the other two down on the table. Do not look at your hands at any time.

No coin on the table. Act surprised. Take up each napkin and shake it out.

SECOND NAPKIN GOES BEHIND FIRST AND IS PUT WITH IT.

The napkins that you use should be square and without frilly edges or printed decorations. When you get them they will have some fold creases, but for this trick you will have to make new folds and creases. Practice a few times making these creases so that you can make them while you are doing the trick.

Fold the *A* edge halfway on the napkin. Make the crease sharp.

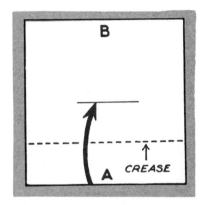

To Bring the Coin Back

A second coin that looks exactly the same as the one you made disappear can be in your trouser pocket, or under a fourth napkin nearby where a secret helper put it and where you find it, or in his pocket where he finds it. The one who finds it must act very much surprised.

Fold the *B* edge down to lie along the center of the folded *A* part.

PASSING COIN FROM ONE FOLDED NAPKIN TO ANOTHER

The second coin having been magically produced is placed on a napkin and folded up in it. A second napkin held by corners is shown on each side, folded like the first, and placed on the table. The first napkin is taken and put on top. A magic signal is made and coin goes from the folded top into the folded bottom napkin.

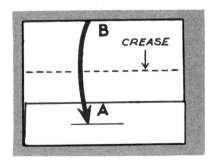

Fold a second napkin the same way so as to have the creases ready.

Fold end *D* to about two thirds of way to *C*.

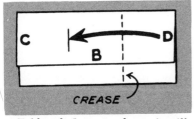

Fold end *C* over as far as it will go. Make crease.

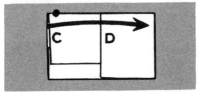

Napkin open showing the new creases and where the coin is to be placed.

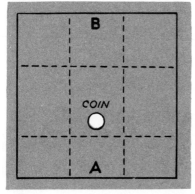

Having placed the coin on the napkin, fold just as you did when making the creases.

Lift up the folded napkin at the top between corners marked *E* and *F* in the sketch. The end *C* will be to the right.

Have somebody feel the coin through the napkin.

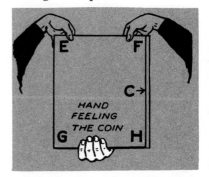

After coin has been felt, move left hand down from *E* to *G*. Tilt the napkin so that the coin will slide into *F* corner where it is felt again. Then move your hand from *G* to *H* corner as shown. Raise the *F* corner and the coin will drop into your hand at *H*.

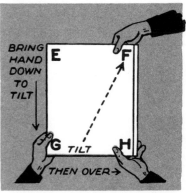

Lay napkin on the table. Take second napkin and placing it flat on the table, fold near end over and leave coin under it. Slide hand out and continue with folding. When making last fold of end *C*, lift it a little bit so that the coin will slide toward the center. Be careful not to let the coin make any sound. All this folding is to be done with napkin on the table.

Take the first napkin which everybody will think is folded around the coin and put it on top of the second napkin that has the coin.

Tell your audience that you will give three magic taps to the top napkin and make the half dollar go into the bottom napkin. Give three taps and open out the napkins.

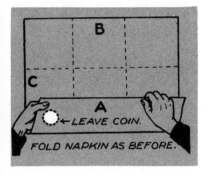

FOLD NAPKIN AS BEFORE.

COIN FROM NAPKIN INTO A BUN

This may end the "three napkins" trick, be a trick by itself, or be the beginning of another trick.

To continue with the napkins, you take one of them and shake it over a bun. Then you break the bun open, take the coin out, and show it.

At Scout dinner parties there are usually a lot of buns on the tables. At your table one of these buns has been "fixed" for your trick. If it is not too big for you to hide in your hand, a half dollar is the best size

for most coin magic. To fix the bun just push the coin up through the bottom as shown here.

PUSH COIN ALL THE WAY IN.

BREAK OPEN AT THE TOP.

Secretly fix the bun while people around the table are busy talking. Quietly take a bun down onto your lap and push the coin through the bottom. Then quietly put the bun back with the other buns. Do not be in a hurry, but to make sure you get your bun, start passing them around. Take the fixed one for yourself and put it on your plate.

You may have a secret friend fix your bun and pass the others around as he keeps his thumb on yours so that nobody but you will take it.

Do not be in a hurry. Wait until you get the people at the table to look your way as you say something like "I wonder if I got a lucky bun this time." Near the end of the party most of the buns will be gone, but your secret friend may keep the fixed bun for you. Look around and ask if there are any buns left, saying that you want to do some magic. Your friend then gives you his bun with the coin in it. Break the top, take out the coin, and give it to your friend.

COIN VANISHES FROM HANDKERCHIEF HELD BY AN ASSISTANT FROM YOUR AUDIENCE

Place a half dollar on the handkerchief spread on a table as shown.

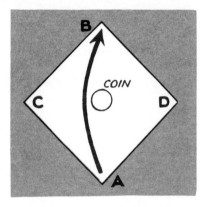

Fold the corner *A* over on corner *B*.

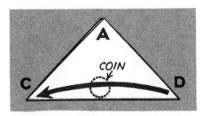

Fold the corner *D* over on corner *C*. Then roll the *C, D, E* end up towards the corner *A*, but do not roll it all the way. The roll must not be made too tight.

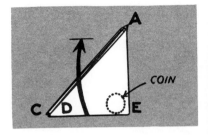

The handkerchief will look like this when rolled. The *C* and *D* corners will be sticking out.

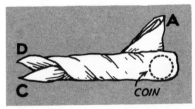

Ask somebody to take the *C* and *D* corners one in each hand, lift the handkerchief from the table, and draw the corners apart as far as they will go. The coin will seem to have vanished.

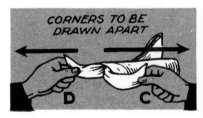

The coin will really be in a groove in the handkerchief at the center. Put your hand over where the coin is and take it and the handkerchief away and put both in your pocket.

Another way to end is to take

both corners and raise one of them. The coin will slide into the lower hand. Hold the corners and shake out the handkerchief. Put it and the coin into your pocket.

COIN VANISHES FROM FOLDED PAPER

Cut a piece of writing paper to five inches square. Put a half dollar or a quarter in the center. Fold paper two-thirds of the way up to cover the coin.

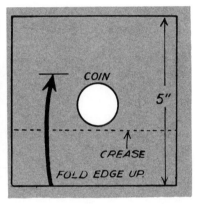

Keep the coin in place and fold one of the sides of the paper back away from you. Fold the other side back also.

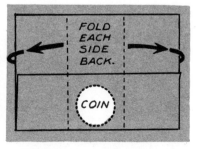

Fold the top part back.

Hold coin in place and raise the paper to be seen. Hold with left hand and point with the right. You may say, "Safe as in the bank."

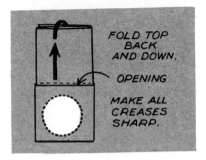

Take the open top with the right hand. Turn the opening down and the coin will slide into this hand. Keep the back of your hand to your audience, do not look at the coin and DO NOT LET IT DROP. Take away the folded paper with your left hand and place it on the table. Have a short pencil in your right trouser or coat pocket.

Put your right hand in the pocket to get the pencil that you may call your "magic wand," and leave the coin in your pocket.

Tap the paper a couple of times with the pencil and tell the coin to go. Open the empty paper and tear it up.

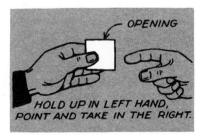

Get the pencil and coin ready in your hand, as shown, before taking your hand out of the pocket.

To bring the coin back again takes a bit of practice, but the moves are not very difficult.

Do not perform until you are sure there will be no slips. One magical way is with a matchbox. A second way is with an envelope.

Have a small matchbox in your pocket with the pencil. When you put the coin in your pocket leave it with the pencil and take out the matchbox. Shake out all of its few matches on the table. Show the empty box saying, "This is my bank safe." Put the two parts of the box beside the folded paper that the audience thinks holds the coin. Take up the paper and say that you are going to put your money in the safe. Put the folded paper into the box and put on the cover. Now say that the lock has snapped and if you want to get your money you must use a key.

Put the pencil on the table and with your left hand pick up the box. Put it into the right hand on top of the coin. The coin will be hidden by the left hand and box while you do this. With your left hand pick up the pencil and say that it is a magic key that will get your money from the box in a magic way.

Touch the box twice and put the pencil down. With the left hand take the box away and show the half dollar in your right.

Open the box and show that the folded paper is empty. Tear up the paper.

Prepare an envelope by cutting off a very thin strip along the edge down to one of the lower corners so as to get a slit. The slit ought to be a little longer than a side of the folded paper. Have this envelope on the table with a few unprepared envelopes. The extras are for people who like to pick up things to try and find out how tricks are done. Pick up the envelopes, take the prepared one, and put the others back on the table. Open the flap and put the folded paper all the way to the bottom of the envelope. The important part is to have the folded paper's opening in line with the slit in the envelope.

Seal the envelope and, holding it flat, let some person feel the coin. When it has ben felt you may hold the envelope up to a light so that all may see the shape of the folded paper.

When doing this, be sure to keep the bottom of the envelope down.

Now take the envelope in your right hand and turn it as shown. Hold the paper and coin in place

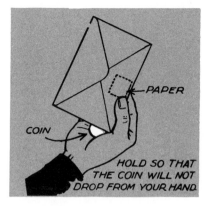

HOLD SO THAT THE COIN WILL NOT DROP FROM YOUR HAND.

for a moment and then loosen your hold. The coin will drop through the opening and the slit into your hand.

Move your hand up a bit and hold envelope level. Ask somebody to hold his hand out flat under it. When ready, flick or snap a finger of your other hand on the envelope and drop the coin from your hand into his. Tear off the slit end of the envelope, take the paper out, open it and tear it up.

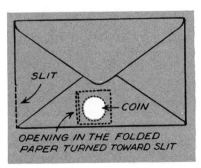

OPENING IN THE FOLDED PAPER TURNED TOWARD SLIT

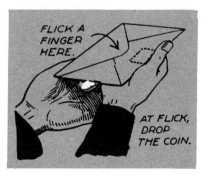

FLICK A FINGER HERE.

AT FLICK, DROP THE COIN.

47

COIN THROUGH A DRINKING GLASS AND PLATE

For some tricks it is better to borrow a coin. In the "coin from envelope," the coin had better be dropped into the hand of its owner. For this trick you will need two coins of your own.

Spread a handkerchief out flat and at its center fasten one end of a short white thread either by a stitch or by a small bit of cellophane tape. To the other end, which should not go beyond the handkerchief edge, fasten a half dollar or a quarter as shown in the drawing. On the underside of a small bread plate stick a coin similar to the one on the handkerchief thread. It can be stuck with a small bit of soap that you moisten. If you are putting on a show at a table by yourself, have the coin already stuck. Also have a drinking glass on the table. If you are at a party you may have a bun on the plate.

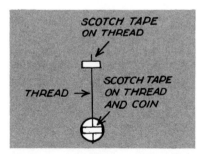

SCOTCH TAPE ON THREAD

THREAD →

SCOTCH TAPE ON THREAD AND COIN

Have the handkerchief in your breast pocket with the center sticking up as shown in the picture. If you are seated at a party table and have not been able to fix the coin to the plate beforehand, have your bit of soap stuck under the edge of the table. While your friends are busy talking, get a coin from your trouser pocket and put it on your lap. Slide your plate a bit beyond the edge of the table, get the soap and fix the coin to the plate. You may be able to get the plate to your lap without being noticed or even slide the coin, without sticking it, under the plate while it is on the table.

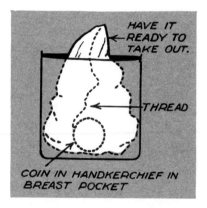

HAVE IT READY TO TAKE OUT.

THREAD

COIN IN HANDKERCHIEF IN BREAST POCKET

When the plate and coin are ready, quietly put the plate back on the table and place the bun back on it. If you do the "coin from bun" trick, put the half dollar into your left trouser pocket.

Take the handkerchief and hold it for a moment as shown, saying that you are going to get your half dollar. With your right hand bring the handkerchief down to cover your trouser pocket. Put your left hand into the pocket and, taking it out empty, get hold of the coin hanging on the thread.

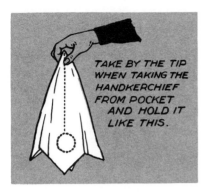

TAKE BY THE TIP WHEN TAKING THE HANDKERCHIEF FROM POCKET AND HOLD IT LIKE THIS.

Bring both hands up and let a bit of the coin be seen.

THREAD

Bring the coin up into the handkerchief so that the right hand can take hold of it through the cloth. Remove the left hand and, sliding the plate a little bit to get it in front of you, put the glass on the plate. Say that you are going to try to pass the coin through the glass onto the plate.

Hold coin over the glass. With left hand drape the handkerchief.

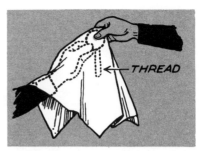

THREAD

GLASS

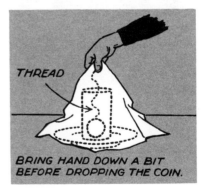

THREAD

BRING HAND DOWN A BIT BEFORE DROPPING THE COIN.

When all is ready you may say that you have to use a very powerful magic word to make the coin go

COMING UP, THE COIN MUST NOT TOUCH THE GLASS.

through the glass onto the plate. The word can be your den number spelled backwards or your Den Mother's or den chief's name.

Say the word and let the coin drop into the glass. All will hear the clink.

Raise the handkerchief straight off the glass so that the coin will not hit against it.

Hold the glass close to the bottom and pick it up. Look at the plate as if surprised and then look into the glass. Turn it upside down to show that the coin has gone. While doing this, put the handkerchief in your pocket. Put the glass down and say that your magic word was too strong and that it must have sent your coin through the plate as well as the glass. Lift the plate on your side only, keeping the other side on the table. Lift only high enough to allow you to put your hand under to take out the coin. You may do this trick without the plate and if asked where the coin has gone, take the second coin from your trouser pocket.

Do not repeat this trick at the same party.

FIRST LOOK AT THE PLATE

THEN LOOK AT THE GLASS.

PUT THE HANDKERCHIEF INTO YOUR POCKET.

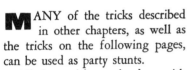

Party Stunts

MANY of the tricks described in other chapters, as well as the tricks on the following pages, can be used as party stunts.

All these tricks can be done with things that are easy to get, such as paper clips, pencils and paper, and paper drinking cups.

Let us start with two clips. With them you will need to have a dollar bill. If you do not have a bill a friend may lend you one, or you can use instead, a piece of half-inch wide ribbon not more than eight inches long.

THE CLIP-JOINING JUMP

Fold the bill into three parts and clip each fold with the corner near-

est to it, as shown. Take the top corners *A* and *B* between your thumbs and fingers. Pull the bill out straight. The clips will join with each other and jump off.

TOP VIEW.
BRING THE EDGES
TOGETHER.

A   B

MERICA

MAKE THE FOLDS
SHARP.

THE BLOWN-UP CAP

Have your friends waiting outside the room until they are called in one at a time. You are to sit at a small table or near the corner of a big one. On the table have a wall mirror. The thinner the frame it has, the better. Have your Cub Scout cap on your head.

Each friend who comes in is to be asked to sit facing you. If the table is big, your friend is to sit near your corner. When seated, he or she is to be asked to hold the mirror upright on the table, edgeways between you. Your nose is to be against the frame, and your friend's face is to be in over the frame so that he or she cannot see what happens at the back of the mirror. The pictures show you these positions.

When ready, take hold of your cap with the hand at the back of the mirror. Move your other hand up and down and say, "Watch me trying to fly." The reflection will give you the second arm. When you have done this a couple of times say, "I want you to blow at me. Give a good steady blow." When your

friend blows, lift your cap up a few inches and say, "Blow harder." Lift the cap to the top of the frame. Your friend will see what seems to be your cap going up by itself. This friend is to stay in the room and have fun watching the surprise of the next person called in.

FRIEND'S VIEW

MOVE HAND →

GIVING A LIFT

Have all your friends except two who are to help you wait outside a closed door. You will call them in one at a time, by numbers given to them on slips of paper. The door is to be closed each time a person enters.

On the floor in the center of the room have two thick books, blocks of wood, or bricks across which is a board about two feet long, with the ends sticking out beyond the supports so that each helper can take hold of an end.

When friend No. 1 comes in he is to be asked to stand on the board and to put his hands on your shoulders as you stand facing him. He is to be blindfolded with a handker-

YOUR VIEW

HOLD CAP

chief. A helper may have to be on a chair to tie the blindfold. Each helper is then to take hold of an end of the board.

Tell your friend that he is now going to go up in an elevator. Say, "One, two, three. Up you go." Your helpers are to lift the board not more than two inches and let it down again, but not all the way to the supports.

They are to keep up this lifting and lowering, doing it evenly together.

Bend your knees and keep going down lower and lower, keeping time with your helpers' lifting.

Your friend is likely to become frightened, because he will feel that he is really going high in the air.

Stop the lifting and let your friend stay in the room to see the next person being elevated.

MAGIC RED PENCIL

Have two pencils, one red and one black. Tell your friends that the red is a magic pencil. Also have some sheets of writing paper and a mirror. With the red pencil print the word *tomato* downward as shown here.

Down alongside print *celery* with the black pencil. When printed, show the words in a mirror.

Tomato will not have changed but *celery* will be reversed. You may print downward in the same way— *hot* and *cold*, *mat* and *rug*, *mouth* and *cheek*.

MAGIC RED ADDITION

With the red pencil copy the first two rows of figures EXACTLY as they are shown on page 54. Have them ready and covered by a few sheets of paper. Give one of your friends the black pencil and a paper. Take out your figures and show or read them, asking your friend to write them down and add them.

While this is being done, you

write the answer shown here. In the mirror your sum will show one added to nine to make ten.

UPSIDE DOWN IN MIRROR

Print *choice* in red and *plums* and price in black. If you have friends whose first names are as shown, print these names in red and their last names in black.

Without saying that you are turning the paper over so that the words will be seen upside down in the mirror, show them. Only the red letters will look the same.

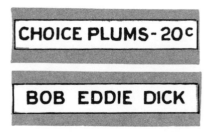

THE TICKING CLOCK

This clock may be drawn with any pencil. If the pencil is red, say that its magic will make the clock tick.

Draw a clock face about two

inches wide. It and its figures do not have to be perfect. Hold the paper as shown between your first and middle fingers having the first finger only in front.

Get thumbnail and the nail of your middle finger together back of the paper. Work nails back and forth. Hold clock to a friend's ear. He will hear the "ticks."

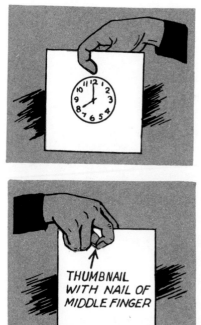

RED AND BLACK DO A FAST DANCE

When you have done the clock and other pencil tricks, say to your friends, "Let me see if there is any more magic left in my red pencil.

If there is, it will make the black one dance."

Wrap a strong rubber band a few times around both pencils at their centers.

Twist the pencils in opposite directions as much as the rubber band will allow. The more twists the better. Put the pencils on the table and let go.

seen easily when the pencil is held in your closed hand.

Instead of a pencil you may use a ruler or light cane. Whichever you use, rub it hard for several seconds against one of your sleeves.

Tell your friends you have to do this to make the pencil magnetic.

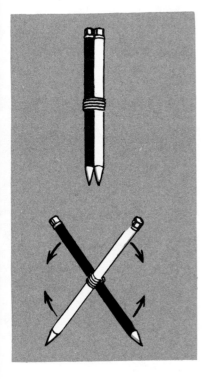

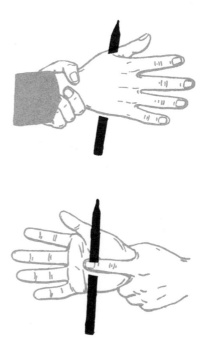

THE MAGNETIZED PENCIL

This trick can be done with the red pencil or any other pencil long enough so that both ends can be

Let your friends see you close the fingers of one hand on the pencil and then turn the back of this hand to them. With the other hand, take hold at the wrist, getting one or two fingertips into the sleeve. Say that you have to hold the hand with the pencil very steady. Slowly open and spread your fingers. The pencil that was held will be seen as though it were sticking to your hand.

The secret: Before you open your hand slide the first finger of the hand holding the wrist onto the pencil.

Let the pencil be seen sticking to your hand for a few seconds and then let it slip down a little bit. Close your fingers on it and slide back the finger that was holding it before you take away the hand that was holding the wrist.

Repeat the sleeve rubbing if asked to do the trick a second time.

CUP MOVING

Place six paper cups in a row on the table. Every second cup is to be upside down as shown.

Two cups that are side by side are to be moved at a time. Only three of these double moves are to be made, and when this has been done, the cups that are turned the same way are to be together in the row.

Give each of your friends a chance to try to make the moves before you do the trick. To show you how, the cups are numbered here.

When you have learned the

LEAVE SPACE ON THE TABLE AT THIS END.

FIRST MOVE: 4 AND 5 TO THE RIGHT OF 6

SECOND MOVE: 1 AND 2 BETWEEN 3 AND 6

THIRD MOVE: 3 AND 1 TO THE RIGHT OF 5

moves, make them quickly so that your friends will find it hard to follow what you are doing. If asked to do the trick a second time, do it in reverse. Move 2 and 3 to the left of 1, 5, and 6 between 1 and 4, and then 6 and 4 to the left of 2. Leave space at the left side of the row for these reverse moves.

CUP TURNING

Place three cups on the table, the middle one upright and the other two upside down. Two cups at a time are to be turned over once so that a cup that was upright will be upside down and one that was upside down will be upright. Only three of these double turnings are to be made. At the end all cups are to be upright. In the drawings the cups are numbered to help you in practicing.

Ask others to try the puzzle before you do it. Give your friends time, because it is not easy. To make it harder for your friends to follow what you are doing, cross your hands when making the second move, taking 1 with the right hand and 3 with the left.

You may do this puzzle in reverse, starting with three cups upright and finishing with the first and third cups upside down. Also you may start with No. 2 down and the others up.

1 2 3
CUPS AT THE START.
TURN 1 AND 2.

1 2 3
1 AND 2 TURNED.
TURN 1 AND 3.

1 2 3
1 AND 3 TURNED.
TURN 1 AND 2.

1 2 3
THREE CUPS NOW UPRIGHT.

Mind Reading

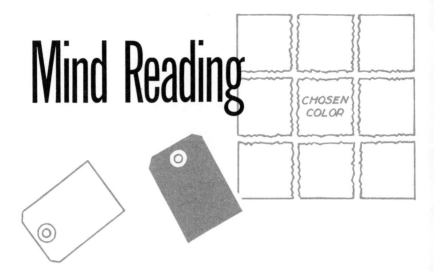

CHOSEN
COLOR

FROM the mind-reading tricks given on the following pages, pick out a few that you think will be the easiest to do and practice them over and over until you can do them well. You will need a helper when you practice and a secret helper for some of the tricks to be done before a lot of people.

Never do more than three or four of the tricks at a time, and never do the same tricks for the same audience unless you learn how to do them in different ways.

Your audience may be one person, a few friends at a party, or a lot of people at a father-and-son dinner.

When doing a mind-reading trick, never be in a hurry to tell what subject is being thought about.

Suppose you have your audience thinking of a ship. Say, "You are thinking of something floating on water. It looks like a boat." Wait a few moments and then say, "It's a big boat. It's a ship."

Suppose red is the color about which your audience is thinking. You see a red dress on somebody. "A lady or girl is thinking of the color of her dress. I would like her to raise her hand." Several hands may be raised. Then say, "I guess the color you are all thinking about is red."

When mind reading you may pretend to be very serious or, if you like, make your act a lot of fun for yourself and your audience.

TELLING THE COLOR OF A TAG

For this trick you will need three package tags of different colors. Get tags that have little cardboard or paper rings around the holes that strings go through. Prepare the tags by loosening the rings on each side of one tag and one ring only on the second tag. Leave the rings on the third tag as they are. Do not loosen the rings too much, just enough so that you can identify the tag by feeling the rings.

Suppose the colors are to be red, white, and blue.

Hold the tags up for all to see and then have a helper take them. While your back is turned, have somebody hold up a tag so that all can see the color. This tag is to be put into your hands, which you are holding behind you.

Turn to face your audience and, keeping your hands at your back, say that you want everybody to think of the color of the tag and that if all think hard enough, you will be able to tell the color they are thinking about.

Of course, you will know the color because you felt the rings.

Do not name the color right away. Pretend you are having a little trouble. Say, "The color is not clear to me. Somebody is not thinking hard enough."

Look puzzled. Then say, "I get it." Wait a moment or two before you name the color.

Practice this trick with your **Den** Mother, den chief, or some other friend.

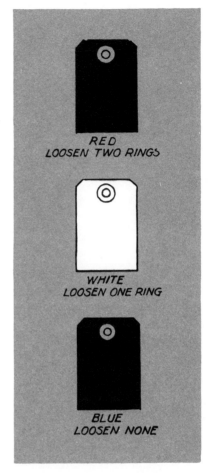

RED
LOOSEN TWO RINGS

WHITE
LOOSEN ONE RING

BLUE
LOOSEN NONE

TELLING THE COLOR OF A CRAYON

Give a box of wax or grease crayons and your Cub Scout cap to anybody in your audience, telling them that a crayon is to be put into the cap while your back is turned.

Somebody is to hold the cap over your head, and everybody except you is to know the color of the crayon.

When the cap is over your head, turn around. If the person holding the cap is between you and the audience ask him or her to stand at either side or behind you. Look at the people and say, "I want all of you to think of the color of the crayon."

Stop a moment and then say, "I hope that the crayon is really in my cap."

Stop again for a moment and say, "Oh, I forgot. The crayon must be pointing the right way."

When you say this, put a hand into the cap and pretend to be fixing the crayon.

As you pretend to fix the crayon, scratch it to get a bit of its color on a fingernail. Bringing your hand

down, get a quick look at the color on your nail. Make sure that the person holding the cap does not see the color on your nail.

When your hand is down say, "O.K., I want you all to think hard of the color, so that I can tell what one you are thinking about." If you missed seeing the color, bring your hand to your forehead as if you were having trouble thinking. When you know the color, bring your hand down and say what the color is.

TELLING RIBBON COLOR

You can tell the color of a ribbon almost the same way you figured out the color of the package tag.

Have three ribbons of different colors. The ribbons must not be less than half an inch in width and sixteen inches long. Like the tags, the ribbons have to be prepared. They are to be cut in slightly different lengths. Let us say that the colors are red, yellow, and green. How to cut them is shown here.

Put and hold one end of the red ribbon under your thumb. This end must be toward the palm of your hand. Bring the ribbon down at the back of your hand, around up over the palm, and then down at the back again. Cut the ribbon where it meets the lower edge of your hand. The yellow is to go around your hand the same way and is cut where it comes to the center of your palm. Cut the green so that the cut end will meet the end under your thumb.

Doing the Trick

Let the ribbons hang from your hand so the lower ends are about even. The upper ends can be covered with your fingers. Give the ribbons to someone in the audience —a secret helper if you like—and ask that a ribbon be given to you when you turn your back. Your hands are to be behind you.

When ready, turn and ask who gave you the ribbon. Look at this person and say, "I want you to think of the color."

While saying this, wrap the ribbon around your hand to get the length that tells the color. Wait a moment or two before naming the color. Make up something to say for each color. If it is yellow, you may say, "Are you thinking of the color of my neckerchief?"

ANOTHER WAY TO PREPARE THE RIBBONS

The three ribbons to be prepared this way are to be not less than two feet long. They are all to be of the same length. Two of them are to be prepared as shown here.

When a ribbon is put into your hands while your back is turned, all

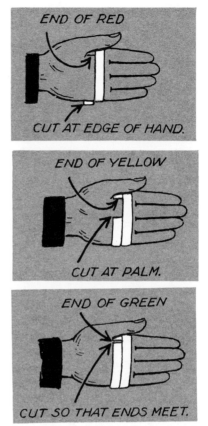

END OF RED

CUT AT EDGE OF HAND.

END OF YELLOW

CUT AT PALM.

END OF GREEN

CUT SO THAT ENDS MEET.

you have to do is to feel one end to know the color. Act as you did while doing the tag trick or the other ribbon trick.

RED

CUT A SLIGHT SLANT AT EACH END.

YELLOW

CUT OFF A CORNER AT EACH END.

GREEN

CUT RIBBON SQUARE AT EACH END.

61

TELLING A COLOR WITHOUT TOUCHING OR SEEING IT

This trick needs lots of practice with a secret helper. Stand behind a chair facing your audience. Have a scarf or handkerchief and ask that someone in the audience come up and blindfold you. Now say that you want somebody to touch something in the room, come forward, sit in the chair, and think of the color of the thing touched. Your secret helper is to do this. When he or she is seated say, "I am going to hold your head and I want you to think hard of the color you touched."

PUT HANDS AT EACH SIDE OF YOUR HELPER'S HEAD.

Put your fingertips on your helper's temples just in front of the ears. All the helper has to do is to grind his or her teeth so that you can feel the squeeze.

Let us say one squeeze for red, two for white, and three for blue. Your helper and you can add other colors, but do not work with too many. The helper should grind his or her teeth slowly.

TELLING THE COLOR OR COLORS OF A MARBLE

A bag or box of marbles of different colors is to be given to your audience. You are to turn your back and when a marble is chosen it is to be put into one of your hands, which you are holding behind you. Make sure that your left hand takes the marble by holding it out. Let everybody see your left hand closing on the marble before you turn around to face them. When you have turned, put the marble into your right hand, close your left, bring it out, and look at it. The back of this hand must be up.

Look at the audience and say that you want whoever gave you the marble to think of its color so that you will know it, too. You may add that if everybody thinks of the color it will be a big help. Then look at your left hand again and keep looking at it.

Now let your right hand with the marble hang down at your side for a moment or two. Bring it up to your forehead as you pretend to be trying hard to learn what the people are thinking.

Move your right hand up and down again, but keep looking at your left hand. You will be able to see the marble as it passes up or down in your right hand. When you know the color, put both hands behind you and put the marble into the left. With right fingers opened wide, give your forehead another rub.

Then say, "I get it," and name the color or colors. You may, if you see the same color in the room and before you name it, say that someone is thinking of the color of his tie or her dress. When you name the color, bring out your closed left hand, open it, and show the marble.

SEEING THE MARBLE IN RIGHT HAND WHILE LOOKING AT THE LEFT

RIGHT HAND IS NOT TO STOP ON ITS WAY UP OR DOWN.

TELLING A WRITTEN COLOR

Give a list of colors, pieces of paper, and a pencil to people seated at a table. Tell them that you want the name of one of the colors written on a paper while you are out of the room. Say that before you are called in, the paper is to be folded a few times, put on the table, and, except for a small bit left sticking out, somebody's hand is to cover the paper. This bit of paper sticking out means nothing, but it adds to the mystery.

When you are back at the table, tell the person whose hand is on the paper to think of the chosen color. You will need a secret helper, and both of you will need lots of practice. Each color on your list is to have a number that must be remembered. Six or seven colors ought to be enough.

Your helper's chair must be opposite yours and his or her feet must be able to touch yours under the table. You are told the color by the number of times your helper's foot is pressed on yours.

The signaling ought to be done slowly so that you will not miss the count. When the number is given, your helper's foot is to give yours a tap sideways.

TELLING WRITTEN NUMBERS

A three-figure number is written on a piece of paper while your back is turned.

The paper is folded a few times or rolled to make a ball or wad and then held up for you to see when you turn around or when you are seated at your table again. Your secret helper lets you know what the number is by pressing on your toe or by grinding teeth as in the color trick on page 62.

There must be a pause between the figures as they are given. During the pause you may pretend you are thinking very hard by closing your eyes or rubbing your forehead.

When you know the number do not tell it right away or in the proper order. First name the middle figure and, after a few moments, say "In front of it, is—." Name the first figure and then tell what the whole number is.

FINDING PAPER WITH NAME OF CHOSEN COLOR

Fold a sheet of square white paper so that you will get nine small squares when the paper is opened. Fold the creases sharply so that the small squares can be easily torn apart. Give the opened paper and a pencil to anybody in your audience. Also give a list of nine colors. Red, orange, yellow, green, blue, purple, brown, white, and black make a good list.

Have the names of the colors printed in large letters so that your audience can see them when held up. The names may be on a long strip or on separate cards. With a few friends at a party your list can be written on a piece of paper. Say that when you turn your back, a color is to be chosen by any person. The person who chooses is to point to the name on the list or hold up the card for all to see. The name of the color is to be written in the center square of the paper and the paper is then to have the names of the other

colors written in the other squares.

When there is a name in each square, the paper is to be torn along the folds into nine pieces and the pieces mixed up. They are to be turned backs up and put on a table or chair near you. Ask all to think of the color.

The name of the chosen color will be on the only square that does not have a straight edge. Pick up any other piece and hold its back to your forehead. Wait a moment and say "Not this color." Repeat a couple of times and then use the center piece. Holding it to your forehead say, "This is the color you are thinking about." Look at paper and name the color.

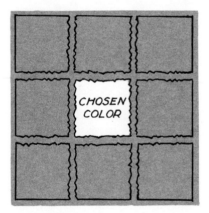

CLOCK FIGURING

Have your den chief or Den Mother or some other friend draw two clock faces for you if you cannot draw them yourself. There are to be no hands, but the center of the face is to have a dot.

the count is the same as the number stopped at on the first count. The two numbers at which the person stopped are to be added. The sum written on the clock will always be fourteen.

Give the clock and a pencil to anybody in your audience. Tell him or her while your back is turned to choose any number and then draw a straight line from it across the center of the clock to another number. The small one is to be subtracted from the big number and the answer written on the face of the clock.

The paper then is to be rolled into a little ball and given to you. You may turn around again.

Take the ball and hold it to your forehead for a few moments and then say "You got six." The subtraction figure will always be six, but don't tell this to your audience.

Give the second clock to anyone except the person who did the subtracting. You will have to show how the counting is to be done. Tell this person to start at 1, count from it the way a clock hand goes, and stop at any number he or she wishes.

When this is done, the count is to start at 1 again, but go back the other way counting 12 as "2," 11 as "3," 10 as "4," and so on until

THE THREE OBJECTS

Place three objects such as a handbook, neckerchief, and a slide in a row on the table. Your assistant— the mind reader—leaves the room and one of the objects is selected by the audience. When the mind reader returns, he immediately points out the object that was chosen. The beauty of this mind-reading trick lies in its simplicity—you can do it without preparation at any time or place.

You simply signal the chosen object to the mind reader this way: If it is the left-hand object, you keep your right hand at your side, but make some slight motion with your *left* hand. You can raise it to your pocket flap and drop it again or put your left hand in your pants pocket.

Another way to signal "left" is to turn your left side toward the mind reader. The right-hand object is signaled in the same way, using your right hand or by turning your right side toward the mind reader.

A simple way to signal the center object is to put both hands in your pants pockets or fold them in front of yourself for a moment—or make no signal at all, left or right.

FINDING A HIDDEN OBJECT

Tell your audience that you have the ability to transfer your thoughts without any difficulty to your assistant—Jimmy Smith—or, better, the Celebrated Wizard from the Upper Heights of Nepal. To prove it, you send him from the room, and someone in your auidence hides a penny or other small object, putting it under a book or a vase or behind a picture.

You call your assistant in. He concentrates deeply to get his "master's" thought waves, then walks directly over to the hidden object and finds it!

What you have done is to show the location of the hidden object by a simple but undetectable trick. When your assistant re-enters the room, you stand with your *right* side toward the hidden object. That is all there is to it. The assistant merely looks at all the likely hiding places in the area indicated. He can nearly always find the hidden object on the first try.

READING THROUGH A WALL

This is a simple but "impossible" mind-reading trick. You present a book to your audience and tell them that you are going to leave the stage. While you are gone, the audience is to choose a page of the book and read the first few lines. You are going to try to pick up the words by mental telepathy!

You go out and one of the spectators calls to you the number of the page that has been chosen; then you ask everybody to concentrate. In a minute or so you call out the first line or two of the chosen page from offstage.

The secret is this: You have two identical paperback books. You hide one in your pocket and allow the audience to choose a page from the other. When the spectators announce the page chosen, you quickly open your copy to that page and read off a line or two in a loud voice.

It is a good idea to give your audience a reason, fair or otherwise, for asking the number of the chosen page. You can say, "Have you chosen a page?" When the answer "Yes" is given, you say, "Don't tell me anything on the page but its number, so I can get its vibrations. Now, think of the number and concentrate on the first two lines. If you all try hard enough, I think I can get the words."

This should be enough to get the spectators to give you the page number without their attaching any importance to it as the secret of the trick.

MIND READING AT A HOME PARTY

You should practice with a secret helper until each of you feels sure that nothing will go wrong when you perform.

At the party there may be friends who want to play games or do stunts. Join in the games, and when a few stunts have been done say, "How would you like me to tell what you are all thinking about!"

Say that you will leave the room and everybody is to think of something in the room. Tell them that they are all to think of the same object and then call you in to tell them what it is.

Just as you are about to leave say, "I would like anybody who has a pen or pencil to point it at different objects when I come back. One of the objects must be what you are all thinking about."

Your helper must lose no time in being first to show you a pen or pencil.

When you come back, tell your helper not to go too fast when pointing. If the object being thought about is small, such as a watch or a button, your helper is to ask, "Is it all right to touch as well as point?" Say "Suit yourself." It may be a big thing not easily pointed at, such as a chair on which somebody is sitting. This must be touched.

How the Trick Is Done

Your helper and you have agreed that the fourth thing pointed at or touched is to be the object being thought about. Suppose it is a clock. Say "no" for the first three things and say "no" for the clock as well. Your helper is to keep on pointing at other objects and you are to say "no" each time. When you have said "no" several times, say "Wait a minute. Somebody is not thinking hard enough. Everybody please think hard about what it is." Your helper is to stop pointing. After a few moments say "I got it. You are thinking about the clock."

If you like, before giving the correct answer you may close your eyes for a short while so that it will seem that you, too, are thinking hard.

It may be some person about whom all agree to be thinking. Your helper will let you know this as you come in by holding the pencil up pointing to the ceiling. Each time a person or an object is pointed at the helper is to raise the pencil after pointing or touching. A few objects are to be pointed at, then the person. After a number of objects and persons have been pointed at, say "Somebody is not thinking hard enough," and so on.

You will know the person being thought about because you and your helper have agreed that it is to be the second person pointed at or touched.

Someone in the audience may say "Let's try again and let me do the pointing." Just say "O.K." and leave the room.

Your helper is to hand over the pencil and say "I'm glad you are doing it this time. My arm is getting stiff." Then he rubs the pointing arm a couple of times. When you come in, stand back far enough to see your helper as well as the things that may be pointed at.

Tell the person now doing the pointing to do it slowly. Your helper is to wait until the first object after the correct one has been pointed at and then he is to rub his arm. Having said "no" six or seven times more, say "Wait a few seconds," and then name the correct object.

Your friends may want you to do more mind reading, and if you want to do it, tell them that you will try it a different way. If you're at your own home, have a couple of sheets of typing paper ready. If at someone else's home, ask for a sheet of paper or have with you a sheet folded the regular way in a long envelope.

Say "When I am out this time, I want somebody to think of any number from one to a hundred and to let everybody know what it is." Show the paper and say, "I want somebody to write the number and a lot of other numbers on this while I am out."

Your secret helper is to write the numbers so that there will be two or three on each piece of the paper when it is torn into nine pieces as described in the "telling colors" trick. The number being thought about is written exactly on the center of the paper with a number above it and another number under it.

When you are called in say, "Don't show me the paper yet. I will turn my back, and I want you to tear the paper into as many pieces as you like." When you are told this has been done, turn around and say, "Please put the pieces of paper on the table or a chair." Pick up one of the pieces and say, "I want everybody to think of the number." Pick up any of the pieces having a straight edge, look at the numbers, hold the paper to your forehead for a moment, and say "None of these." Pick up two or three other straight-edged pieces, do and say the same thing as you did with the first piece. Take the torn-edged piece, hold it to your forehead a little longer than you did the others, smile, and say, "You are thinking about . . ." Wait a moment, and then say the number.

When you have finished, thank everybody for having helped you.

A second way to do the number-telling trick is to have the number written where your helper and you have planned, to be ready for anybody who might hope to find out how you do the trick and ask you to do it again.

All you have to do is to agree that the number be written, let us say, as the third number on the third line. Any place on any line will do, but it is best to use one of the top lines. Five or six lines should be enough. This time, when you come in, take the paper and look at a lot of numbers, hand the paper to anybody, and say "Please look at a few of these numbers. Look at the number everybody is thinking about. Look at a few more numbers and then look at me and think of the number."

Do this with three or four people and then take the paper. Look at several different numbers and then say, "Oh, here it is! Everybody who looked at me was thinking of . . ." Wait a moment and then say what the number is.

If asked to do the trick again, say, "All right, but let's make it short this time." Let everybody pick any number from one to ten, write it on a piece of paper, pass the paper around for everybody to see, and then fold the paper into a ball.

Your helper, whose hands are partly closed near each other, is to quietly slide out the number of fingers or fingers and thumbs that will let you know what the number is. Do not look at the fingers as you come in. Take the paper ball, go to a few people, hold the ball in front of their eyes and say "Please think of the number inside of this." Your helper must be one of the people you go to, but not the first one or the last.

You will learn the number as you glance at your helper's fingers. Hold the ball to your forehead, close your eyes a few seconds as if thinking, open them, smile, and say the number.

MIND READING FOR LAUGHS

These tricks are best suited for parties where there are a lot of people. Of the tricks given here, do no more than five or six at the same party. If called on to do more, do one or two as encores.

These are teamwork tricks to be done by you and a partner. Your partner, who will do most of the work, ought to be a person who knows how to get laughs. A loud voice will help.

At most places where big dinners are held there is usually a platform or stage. Otherwise a table will do as a platform. On the stage or platform there is to be a chair for you.

Except when introducing you, your partner will be on the floor with the audience during most of the act.

Standing beside you on the platform, he should introduce you like this: "Ladies and gentlemen, we are honored this evening by having as our guest, one of the greatest, one of the most amazing, one of the most marvelous mind readers in all the world. Even though blindfolded he will tell you what you see and what you are thinking about. He will tell you your secret thoughts. Ladies and gentlemen, I have the privilege of presenting to you the world renowned (your name). Give him a big hand!"

Give the Cub Scout salute and bow to your partner. He offers you the chair. When you are seated he blindfolds you with a handkerchief and leaves the platform.

Your partner is to ask you a number of questions, and each time you are to wait a moment or two as if thinking before you answer him. At times, after you have answered him, he is to say something like "Marvelous, wonderful, how does he do it?" and so on.

He is to have a closed box and in it a red neckerchief, a bell, a flashlight, and a big pin. He opens the box, takes out the neckerchief, holds it up, and says "I have something here and I would like you to tell what color it is." Before you say anything, he goes on "Are you ready?" When he says "ready," he is to say the first part of the word as loud as he can. You answer "The color is red."

He then asks you what the object he holds is, saying, "You can't skate on it, but you can have a slide on it. Please tell what it is." Your answer is "a neckerchief."

He rings the bell and asks you what he is holding. When you tell him, he asks you to tell in which hand he is holding the bell, saying, "I will give you two chances to tell me." He holds it in his left, but you are to say "right." He waits a moment and then says "Well, you have one chance left. Which hand is it in?" When you say "left," he says "wonderful." Next object shown is the flashlight. Holding it up, your partner says, "The object I have now is not very heavy." You are to ask "Is it very light?" He answers "I will only say it is light and you should be able to say what it is in a flash." You say "You are holding a flashlight." The pin is shown, and

your partner says "What I have now is something small. I will bring it near you so that you will be better able to tell what it is. I may touch you with it." Take time thinking until he pretends to give you a jab. Jump up and shout, "It's a pin." Rub yourself where you are supposed to have been jabbed and then sit down.

Taking a half dollar from his pocket, your helper holds it up and says, "Here is something that is very remarkable because half of it is a quarter. Can you tell us what it is?" When you have told him, he is to say to the audience "A lot of you may think that our great mind reader and I had all this arranged ahead of time, but to prove to you that he can really read minds, I will ask you for some different objects for him to identify." Going to the audience he looks for a person wearing a wrist watch. Putting his hand on the watch he says, "I am now touching something and I would like you to tell us what it is. Don't be in a hurry. Take your time, take your time." When you have said "a watch," he goes to another person and touches an object. Whatever it is, you and he have seen it before you put on your act and have agreed that it is to be the second object. When he touches the object he asks "What is the color of the thing I am touching now?" When you have told the color, your partner is to go to a friend who knows nothing about the act and who agrees to write on a pad given him by your partner. "I bet you can't tell what I have written." The sheet of paper is to be torn off, rolled in a ball, and given to you. Holding it to your forehead for a moment, tell what was written. Your partner then gives the pad to some other person and says, "Please write any number you like between one and a hundred. Fold the paper and give it to me." Bringing the paper to you, he says, so that everybody can hear, "On this paper a person has written a number."

Suppose the number is 37. Your partner tells you that the number is between one and a hundred and then says, "In fact, it is between 36 and 38." After thinking awhile say "The number is 37."

After this, your partner is to say "Let us test him some other way." He goes to the blackboard and writes the letter B and says "Please tell me what letter I have written. Be careful, be careful." When he says B the second time, he says it slowly and clearly.

When you have said "The letter is B," he writes T and says "This letter always starts trouble." Then he writes U and says "What have I written this time? It is not the letter I, so you have your choice of twenty-five other letters." You are to say, "If it is not I it must be you. So the letter is U."

"All right," says your partner, "I will write one more letter that tells what you can't do now." He writes C. After a short pause for "thinking," say "I can't see. You wrote C."

He may end the act by drawing a tree and saying "I don't want to get you out on a limb, but can you tell me what I have drawn?" Say "limb, limb, limb" slowly and then say "You drew a tree." He may draw a square and tell you that it is something with four sides. Say "What you drew has six sides. You drew four sides, but your square has two more sides—the inside and the outside."

Your partner concludes by saying "And now, ladies and gentlemen, our guest has given us a great demonstration of his powers. I will remove his blindfold and I want everybody to give him a big hand."

Stand and give the Cub Scout salute.

Rope and String Tricks

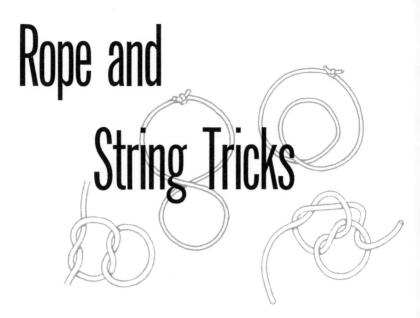

THE best rope for tricks is a white woven cotton rope called "soft rope." Most cities and big towns have stores where equipment for games and tricks is sold. Not all of these stores carry soft rope, but they may be able to tell you where you can get it. A local rope dealer or your Scout trading post also may help get it for you.

For some tricks, clothesline or sash cord can be used if it is not too new. These hard cords are not to be used when cutting has to be done.

If you have soft rope and have cut pieces that you want to use a number of times, work some rubber cement into the ends or have your den chief show you how to whip them to prevent the ends from fraying.

For some of the tricks where you are close to your audience and you are using string, use the white string that you can get at most any hardware, stationery, or dime store.

The heavier or thicker this string is, the better. Before performing with it, get all the kinks out of the pieces you will use by pulling them back and forth over the edge of a table.

For cutting tricks, your scissors will have to be sharp and when doing the tricks you will have to be careful.

THE UNDERHAND OVERHAND KNOT

Take a piece of rope three feet

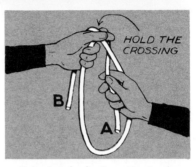

BACKS OF HANDS
TOWARDS THE FLOOR

HOLD THE ROPE
BETWEEN THUMBS
AND FIRST FINGERS.

A

B

long and hold it with both hands as shown here. Hold it about six inches from each end.

Bring the B end over the A end on left first finger. Close left thumb on where the ends cross.

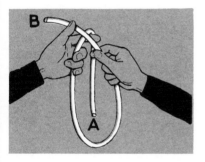

B

A

Hold the crossing firmly with left thumb and finger. Remove right hand and let the ends hang down.

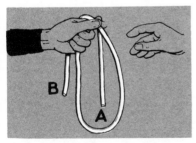

B

A

Put right hand into the loop now made and take hold of the end A. Do not let go of the crossing.

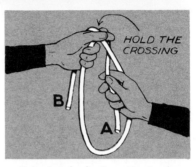

HOLD THE
CROSSING

B

A

Bring A back through the loop and pull until you have what looks like a small knot.

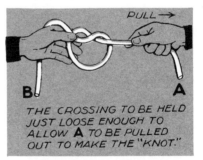

PULL →

B

A

THE CROSSING TO BE HELD
JUST LOOSE ENOUGH TO
ALLOW A TO BE PULLED
OUT TO MAKE THE "KNOT."

Left thumb still holding the crossing against the first finger, the "knot" is shown to all. Close your left hand on the fake knot and turn the back of this hand up. Let the end A go to bring your right hand over to take the end B. Give the end B a pull and then pull the rope on the A side as though you were

THE "KNOT" GETS SMALLER AS THE
ROPE IS BEING PULLED OUT.

B

SHOWING THE CROSSED PART
HELD BY THE LEFT THUMB

A

making the overhand knot tight. The left thumb is no longer holding, and what you are really doing is pulling the crossing out straight.

With your right hand tap the back of your left and say that you are making the overhand knot into an underhand one.

Put right hand beside the left and holding the rope, slide both along to opposite ends. The "knot" will have disappeared.

THE "IS NOT" KNOT

With your three-foot piece of rope make an overhand knot in the center of the rope as shown in the picture. Do not pull it tight, but leave an open loop like the one shown here marked C.

Make another knot the reverse of the way you made the first one. You will get a second loop marked here as D. This loop must also be left open like C.

Take end A down and bring it through loop C from the FAR side toward yourself.

Take A up again and now bring it through loop D from the FAR side, again toward yourself.

Holding end B in the left hand and end A in the right, slowly draw the ends out until there is only a small bit of a knot on the rope. Blow on this and at the same time give an extra pull. The knot will disappear and you will be holding a straight rope. You may say that this is the "is not" knot.

After practicing a few times with the rope on a table you will be able

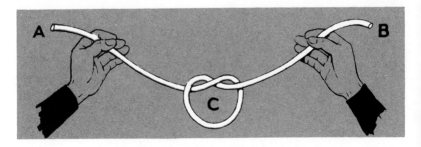

A

B

C

to do this trick with the rope held up in your hands.

If you find it easier to use the end B instead of A, put B through loop C from your side and away from you, then up and through loop D from your side and again away from you. When A and B are pulled apart the knot will disappear. For more fun, try this trick both ways.

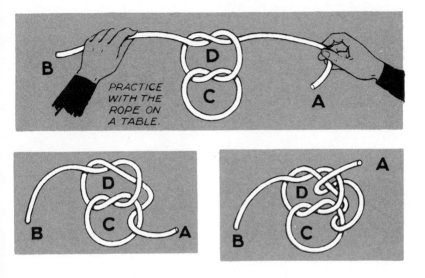

PRACTICE WITH THE ROPE ON A TABLE.

ANOTHER DISAPPEARING KNOT

Hold both ends of your three-foot rope in your left hand. Put your right hand under and through the bend.

TWO LOOPS ARE FORMED.

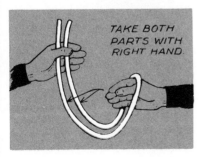

TAKE BOTH PARTS WITH RIGHT HAND.

Bring your right hand holding the two rope parts back through the bend to make the two loops as shown here.

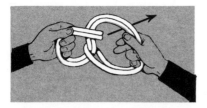

Put the ends in your left hand through both loops. Let go with the left and take hold of one end.

Take the other end in your right hand and pull ends apart. When small knot forms blow on it and pull the rope straight.

← PULL SLOWLY →

"CAN YOU MAKE IT" KNOT

Ask anybody to take the ends of your three-foot rope, one end in each hand, and without letting the ends go, make a knot in the middle. When this person fails, show him how it can be done. Ask him to hold

the rope leaving the ends free for you to take.

First fold your arms and then take the rope ends as shown here.

Unfold your arms and the knot is made. You may have to shake it off your wrists.

Another way to make the knot is to hold one end and then put the rope over your arm so that a loop will hang down on the side nearest you. The other end is to hang down at the far side as shown.

Put your free hand through the loop and take hold of the end hanging down. Bring your hand and the end back through the loop. Lower your hands so that the loop will drop off your arm. The knot is made. Do not pull the knot tight.

close to the loop and beyond it. Get the part of *A* that was below your hand in between thumb and finger holding the loop. Quickly pull *A* back toward yourself. It will catch with the loop and look as if it had been threaded through.

SPEED KNOTS

To make the speed knots you must first have your rope ready in your hands as shown in the pictures. Do not tell anybody what you are going to do until you have the rope in position.

You may, if you like, give a second piece of rope or string to some person and ask him to see if he can make a knot as fast as you can. Both of you are to start when you finish counting to three and say "go."

When you have given him the rope and while you are talking to him, you can be getting your rope in position without looking at it and without the other person noticing what you are doing.

THREADING THE LOOP

Hold your rope or a string three feet long in the crotch of your left thumb as shown here.

Take *B,* the part nearest you, and wrap it around your thumb two or three times and then bring it up to make a loop held between thumb and first finger.

With right hand take *A* not more than two inches from the end, bring it up and point it at the loop. Make a few pokes as if you were going to put it through the loop. Keep your left first finger pointing out straight.

Make another poke, but this time

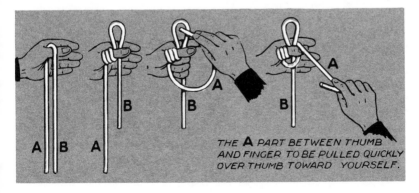

THE **A** PART BETWEEN THUMB AND FINGER TO BE PULLED QUICKLY OVER THUMB TOWARD YOURSELF.

Left hand holds the rope at the center. Right hand holds both ends. Left hand is to turn inwards as shown by arrow.

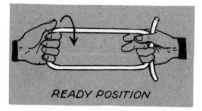

READY POSITION

Turned left hand in a small loop goes through to take top part of the loop held by the right hand. Arrow shows where to take loop.

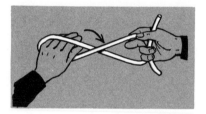

The left hand takes the part back through the loop as the hands are brought closer together.

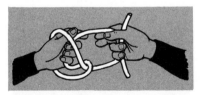

Left hand draws the rope back through the loop to form the knot.

From the start to the finish there should be no stop in the moves. With practice, your time for making the knot should be not much more than a second.

ANOTHER QUICK ONE

Another speed knot, which might be called "the world's fastest knot," is also made from a "ready position," but getting the rope into position and making the knot should be done as one move. After a little practice you will find this speed knot easy.

Take the rope in your left hand about seven inches from the end marked *A*. Slide your right hand along the rope to about seven inches from the end *B*.

Turn right hand inward to bring palm up.

Bring your hands close together. End *B* will hang in front of right and end *A* at back of left hand. Spread any two fingers on each hand.

Bring your right hand behind your left and with spread fingers take *A* part of the rope. Take *B* part with the left fingers.

When your fingers have taken the end parts of the rope, separate your hands as quickly as you can to make "the world's fastest knot."

RIGHT HAND HOLDING THE
ROPE TO TURN PALM UP.

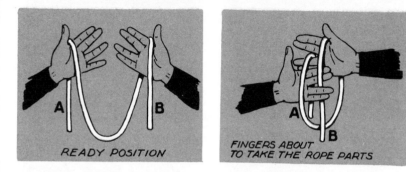

READY POSITION

FINGERS ABOUT
TO TAKE THE ROPE PARTS

THE TWIN KNOTS

With left hand hold the ends of your rope and have your first finger in between them. Put right hand under the bend in the rope to take hold of both *A* and *B*.

Bring back the right hand so that the rope will form two loops. Bring part of the loop made by *A*, which is on the side nearest you, a little way through *B*.

Bring left hand over so that the

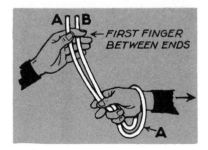

A B
← FIRST FINGER
BETWEEN ENDS

A

end *A* can be taken between the right hand middle and third fingers.

Holding the ends, draw hands apart but not too quickly. As if by magic two knots will suddenly appear on the rope.

over toward the left as shown by the arrow. This turn will make a loop on the rope.

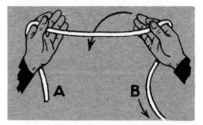

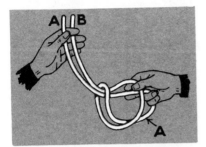

Bring the loop over the fingers of the left hand. Let the loop be loose.

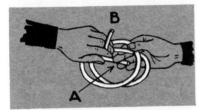

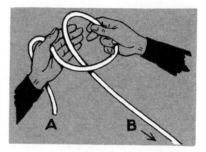

Bring right hand back to make second loop to go on left hand with the first.

LOTS OF KNOTS

For this trick you will need a piece of rope or string six or seven feet long. It should have no kinks.

With left hand palm up, hold the rope about six inches from one end. With your right hand palm up, take hold seven or eight inches from the left hand. Turn your right hand

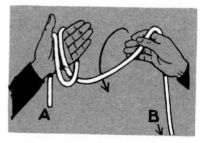

Keep on making as many loops as your left hand can take or rope will allow.

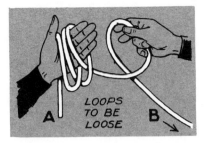

LOOPS
TO BE
LOOSE

A   B

Put right hand through the loops and take hold of the *A* end at back of left.

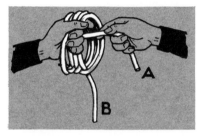

A

B

Holding *A* end, take the loops from your left hand and put them on a table.

THE LOOPS MAY BE PLACED IN A HAT.

A

B

Slowly pull end *A* up. There should be as many knots as there were loops.

Another way to make the knots appear is to hold both the loops and the end *A* in one hand and then,

holding the end only, throw the looped rope as far as you can.

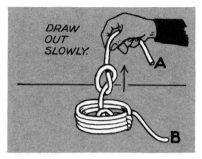

DRAW
OUT
SLOWLY.

A

B

TIED, FREED, TIED

A member of your audience is invited to tie your wrists together with a short piece of rope. He may pull the rope tight and make as many knots as he wishes.

When your wrists are tied you turn your back for a second, wave a free hand for everybody to see, turn around again, and show that your wrists are still tightly tied together.

Left hand palm up. Place the center of the piece of rope across your wrist at an angle in the direction of

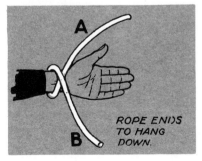

A

B

ROPE ENDS
TO HANG
DOWN.

A as shown. Let both ends hang down. Bring *B* around under your wrist and then across over *A*.

Right hand back up. Put your right wrist on top of the rope where it is crossed. Ask somebody to take the rope ends and tie them as tightly as possible on top of your right wrist. The ends are to be just long enough to tie.

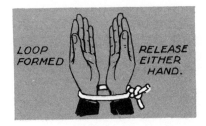

LOOP FORMED   RELEASE EITHER HAND.

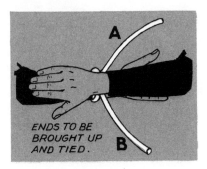

ENDS TO BE BROUGHT UP AND TIED.

Turn your back to your audience and swing both hands around as shown by the arrows. Your palms will come together and the rope will make a single loop.

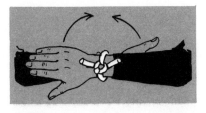

Take one hand out of the loop and wave it. Put it in the loop again and swing your hands back to the position in picture No. *3*. Turn around and have the knots untied.

A PRISONER ESCAPE WITHOUT UNTYING KNOTS

You and a friend are supposed to be war prisoners tied together with ropes on your wrists. You and he are also tied separately with ropes going in opposite ways to heavy or fixed objects that neither of you can move. The first part of the escape is to free yourself from your friend, and the second part is getting free from the objects to which both of you are tied.

Both parts may be done if you are putting on a show either indoors or outdoors. When doing both parts of the escape your friend and the person who ties the knots must know how the trick is done.

If doing the first part only, where neither you nor your friend are tied to objects, nobody but yourself need know how the escape is done. Let your friend try for a while before you show how you free yourself from him without opening a single knot.

You might also have several tied couples in a contest to see which two can become separated first.

ARM ROPE TIED TO ANY FIXED OBJECT. ALLOW SLACK.

ROPE TO THE OBJECT MAY BE TIED TO EITHER ARM.

your friend's hand, beyond and then under his wrist loop.

Pull your rope through, spread it out and bring it over your friend's hand to the palm side.

YOUR FRIEND'S HANDS

CROSS THE ROPES THIS WAY.

YOUR HANDS

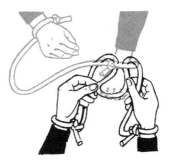

On the palm side pull your rope down through the wrist loop again. The ropes will be separated.

YOUR ROPE TO GO UNDER WRIST LOOP AS SHOWN BY ARROW.

Loop to be just tight enough to keep hands from pulling through. Bring center of your rope over

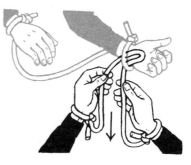

The second part of the "prisoner escape" is done when you and your friend are separated. He, as well as you, must know how to get free from the rope tied to an object. The person who ties the ropes on the arms must know that the loops he makes are loose enough to be moved down from the arms to the wrists. The rope tying your arm to the object may be on either arm. The way to free yourself from this rope is practically the same as the way you separated your wrist rope from your friend's.

Bring arm loop down and pass as much of it as you can under the wrist loop and then over your hand. The arrows show the way.

Having passed over your hand, the arm loop is to be pulled back through the wrist loop as shown here. This will free you from the object.

When all of the separations have been made, the person who tied the knots is then asked to untie them. If you are having contests, you, of course, may be the person to do the tying.

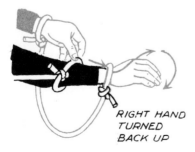

RIGHT HAND
TURNED
BACK UP

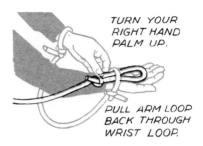

TURN YOUR
RIGHT HAND
PALM UP.

PULL ARM LOOP
BACK THROUGH
WRIST LOOP.

ROPES THROUGH YOUR WAIST

For this trick you will need two pieces of rope each about six feet long. They are to be tied together at their centers with a small piece of easily broken thread. When tied, bend the ropes away from each other as shown on following pages.

Nobody in your audience must know about the ropes being tied, and everybody must be seated in front of you. Have your prepared ropes with a few other pieces on a table or hanging over the back of a chair. The tied part must be out of sight. You will need two helpers who are to stand one on each side a few feet away, also a little bit in front of you so that they will not be able to see your back. They need not be Cub Scouts.

Do not say what you are going to do until everything is ready. Having asked two people to come up and having shown them where to stand, take up your two ropes keeping the tied part hidden in your right hand.

When you drop the B parts bring the ropes, with your right hand hiding the tied part, to back of your waist where you again grasp the B

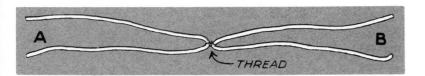

A — THREAD — B

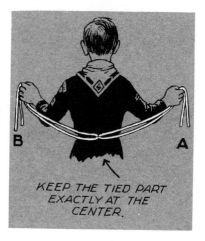

RIGHT HAND HIDES THE TIED PART.

B

WITH THE LEFT HAND LIFT THE B PARTS UP HIGH FOR A MOMENT AND THEN LET THEM DROP.

A

KEEP THE TIED PART EXACTLY AT THE CENTER.

the ropes and bring them around each side to the front. Be sure to keep the tied part from being seen.

Give one of the ends of A to one helper and one of the ends of B to the other.

Cross the second parts of A and B, tie them to make a loose single knot and then give an end to each helper. Now say that you are going to make the rope come through you. Ask your helpers to keep a good grip on the ropes and pull hard when you say "Now." When pulled, the thread will break and both ropes will come free in front of you. They will seem to have come through you as you step back.

Another way to do this trick is to get a person with a coat as a third helper. Bring the ropes around his waist under his coat, which should be open in front. The helpers who are to hold the ropes will not be able to see the thread-tied part.

When putting the ropes around your third helper stand in front of him. Put your right hand that holds and covers the tied part under his coat and around to the back of his waist at the middle. Put your left hand around the other side under the coat and get hold of the two parts of the bent A rope. The right hand without letting go is to slide onto the two parts of the B rope.

parts securely in your left hand.

With the tied part at the center of your back slide both hands along

STAND ASIDE BEFORE YOU
TELL YOUR HELPERS TO PULL.

Slide both hands along the ropes and bring the ends to the front. Give the two ends of *A* to the helper at the left and the ends of *B* to the other helper at the right. Ask these helpers to hold the ropes for a mo-ment. Tell everybody that you will tie one of the ropes around the third helper and that, by magic, you will make both ropes come through him. Joke with the audience and say that the trick will not upset him.

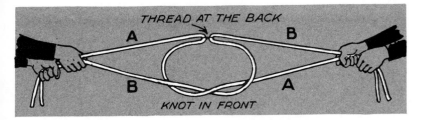

THREAD AT THE BACK

A

B

B

A

KNOT IN FRONT

Take one end from each side helper and tie them in a single knot as already described.

This picture shows how the ropes go around the waist and are tied in front. When the rope is tied, give an end back to each helper as shown here. Standing to one side give the word to pull or, asking the side helpers to keep a good grip, tell the roped helper to take a couple of steps backward.

little way down under your shirt collar so that it cannot be seen.

Keep pushing the rope down around each side of your neck until your hands meet at the back. Then bring the ends forward and let them hang down, one over each shoulder.

The dotted lines in the picture show the part of the rope pushed down around your neck into your shirt collar.

TIED ROPE THROUGH YOUR NECK

Nobody is to be behind you when you do this trick. It is very easy to do, but it needs a little bit of advance preparation. The trick also requires that you come into a room or onto a stage facing your audience. When you enter, the audience sees what they think is a piece of rope around the back of your neck with the ends hanging down in front, one end over each shoulder. The rope ought to be about six feet long.

Say that you are going to tie the ends together, pull the knot tight, and try to make the tied rope come through your neck.

Put the center of the rope in FRONT of your neck and push it a

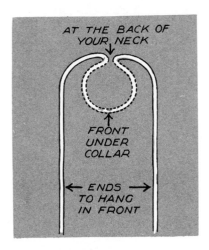

AT THE BACK OF YOUR NECK

FRONT UNDER COLLAR

← ENDS →
TO HANG
IN FRONT

Take the rope ends and tie a single knot as shown here. Take the ends, one in each hand close to the knot.

You may say that you are a little bit afraid of this trick because you might take your head off if you pulled the knot too tight.

Put your head back so that everybody can see the knot. Suddenly yank the rope forward and stretch it out. The knot will be there and the rope will seem to have come through your neck.

ROPE LOOP THROUGH YOUR NECK

Tie the ends of a six-foot piece of rope or cord so as to make a loop. Stretch the loop and put a thumb in the bend at each end. Get the knot to the center away from each thumb.

Lift the loop over your head and bring its ends (*A* and *B*) to the front over your shoulders. Because the rope has to be snapped off very quickly, have it outside your neckerchief as shown here, instead of having it against your neck.

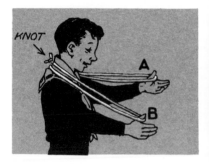

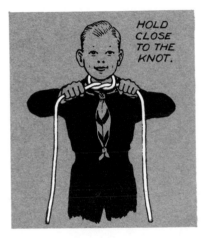

Bring hands together and put right thumb up through end *A*. Take out left thumb and then put it back up through both ends along

How rope with knot will look after coming through.

the right thumb. When doing this, have your fingers hide the moves. Now spread hands apart.

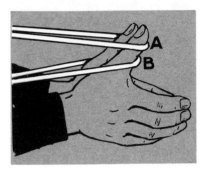

As you spread your fingers have your first fingers and thumbs take hold of the top or *A* end of the loop. Hold the *B* or lower part with your other fingers. The rope is made longer in the drawing than it should be so that you can see the grips better.

Tilt your head back so that the rope looks as if it were looped twice around your neck. Keeping a good grip on the lower *B* part with both hands, suddenly let go of the *A* part, held by the first fingers and thumbs, as you snap your hands forward and as far apart as the loop

will go. The loop will seem to have come through your neck.

DOUBLE-LOOPED CORD THROUGH FINGER (FIRST METHOD)

Tie a piece of cord or string two and a half or three feet long to make a loop. At the side opposite the knot give the loop a twist so that part of the left-hand side, *A*, will cross over the *B* side as shown below.

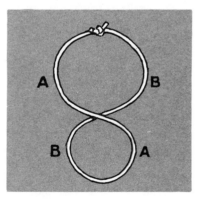

Turn the lower loop over into the upper. The *B* side will then be crossing over the *A*. The crossing part marked *C* in the picture is to be held by your teeth. Hold the knot end in your left hand.

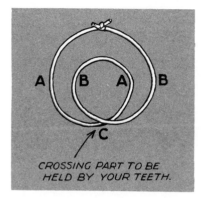

A   B   A   B

↑C

CROSSING PART TO BE
HELD BY YOUR TEETH.

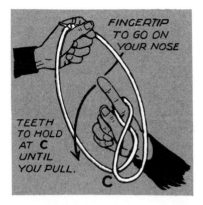

FINGERTIP
TO GO ON
YOUR NOSE

TEETH
TO HOLD
AT C
UNTIL
YOU PULL.

C

With the crossing C hidden in
your mouth and your left hand holding the knot end, bring your right
hand under the B side of the outer
loop and put your first finger down
through the inner loop. Then swing
it up.

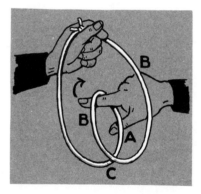

B

B

A

C

Put tip of turned up finger on
your nose. Pull the outer loop taut.
Suddenly let go with your teeth as
you pull the cord free with your
left hand. Be sure to keep your finger on your nose for a couple of
seconds after the pulling.

DOUBLE-LOOPED CORD THROUGH FINGER (SECOND METHOD)

Arrange the loops and hold with
the teeth and left hand as shown
in the first method. Bring the right
hand under and put your right first
finger up through the inner loop.
Bring this loop out under right side
B of the outer loop.

Holding at C with your teeth,
pull both loops taut. Bring your first
finger over the B side of the outer
loop and then under the A side.

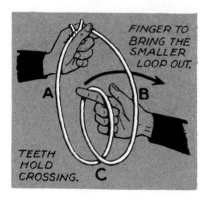

FINGER TO
BRING THE
SMALLER
LOOP OUT.

A   B

TEETH
HOLD
CROSSING.   C

Put the fingertip on your nose and wait a moment. Pull quickly, keeping your finger on your nose.

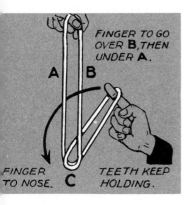

FINGER TO GO OVER **B**,THEN UNDER **A**.

A B

FINGER TO NOSE. C

TEETH KEEP HOLDING.

LOOPED STRING THROUGH YOUR HAND

Use the same loop as for the "through finger" trick.

Put the loop on a table or on your knee if you are sitting down. Take the far side and bring it over the near side to get two loops as shown. Make sure that the D-A side crosses over the C-B.

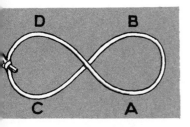

Place your left hand on the crossed part. With the right hand take up the A part, bring it over B and around under your left fingers so that they will be in a loop.

Keep your left hand flat and with your right bring the A-B loop over on the back of the left. Raise your fingers a little when you are putting the A part of the loop under them.

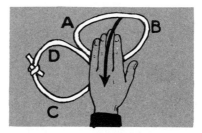

Bring the part C under D, around and under your fingers on the thumb side.

Bring this second loop onto the back of your flat hand also.

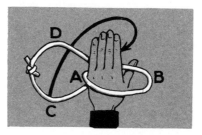

Keep your hand pressing down on the string parts under it so that they will not slip out. Your left thumb can help hold them.

91

These parts are no longer crossed. With your right, take hold of what looks like a loop on the back of your left hand. Lift it up a bit and get ready for the pull.

LEFT HAND TO KEEP PRESSING. RIGHT TO GRIP LOOP.

Pressing with your left hand, with your right give what seems to be a few hard tugs. Keeping your fingertips in place, raise the palm of your hand the least little bit and give the cord a hard yank. The loop will seem to come through your hand that you must still keep flat for a few seconds.

PULL LOOP STRAIGHT UP.

Some of these rope and string tricks should not be done for the same people more than once unless there is a second way of doing them. When asked to repeat tricks, you may say that you would like to perform some other tricks first. However, you may do most of the pull-through string tricks several times.

LOOPED STRING THROUGH A BUTTONHOLE

Using the same loop as for the other tricks, put it through a button hole and hold it as shown. Loop A is near the thumb tip and loop B is well down.

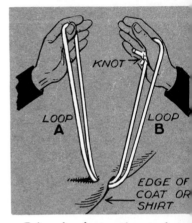

KNOT

LOOP A LOOP B

EDGE OF COAT OR SHIRT

Bring hands together and put loop A on the right thumb with loop B. Hold first finger on the thumb. Have hands closer than shown here.

FINGER ON THUMB

A

B

TURN YOUR LEFT HAND OVER AND TAKE THE STRING PART MARKED BY THE ARROW.

Turn your left hand over, put it under loop *A*, take and draw back the nearest string of the *B* loop. Put left thumb up into the *A* loop and hook it as you turn your left hand back to the first position.

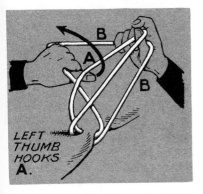

LEFT THUMB HOOKS A.

The loops should now look like this. Spread your hands as far apart as the loops will allow. Suddenly let go of the top part held by your thumbs and first fingers and pull the string free on your thumbs.

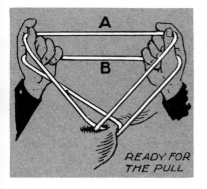

READY FOR THE PULL

LOOP FROM FINGER OF HELPER

Make a tied loop from a piece of cord or string not more than two feet long. Ask somebody to hold up a finger. Put the loop over this finger. Hook a finger of your left hand into the knot part and pull the loop fairly taut. Bring your right hand over, turned palm up and with middle finger as shown.

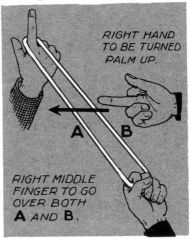

RIGHT HAND TO BE TURNED PALM UP.

RIGHT MIDDLE FINGER TO GO OVER BOTH A AND B.

Having crossed *A* and *B*, turn your right hand halfway over and

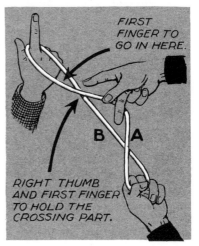

FIRST FINGER TO GO IN HERE.

RIGHT THUMB AND FIRST FINGER TO HOLD THE CROSSING PART.

with middle finger bring *A* back over *B*. Put this finger and your thumb into the opening made. Put first finger into the next opening as shown by arrow. Bring your thumb up to hold the crossed part with your first finger.

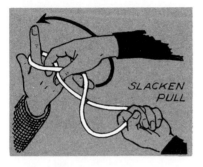

Holding the crossed part, swing your right hand around to bring the middle finger with the *A* part up to go on top of your helper's finger.

Let go with thumb and first finger and pull with your left hand. Your middle finger is to stay on helper's finger for a few seconds.

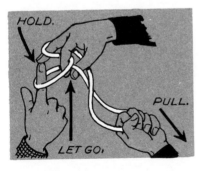

LOOP AND VEST TRICK

A piece of rope or cord four or five feet long is tied to make a loop. A person wearing a vest is asked to take off his coat and be your helper. Put the loop on his right arm and ask him to put his right thumb in his lower vest pocket. He is not to take his thumb out until the trick is finished.

Now ask somebody to try to get the loop free without untying the knot. Then show that it can be done.

Bring the loop end up and put it through the armhole as shown by the arrow. One side of the loop is to go in front of and one side in back of your helper's shoulder.

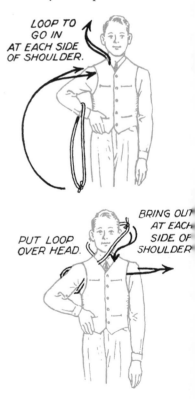

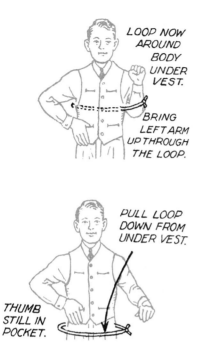

LOOP NOW AROUND BODY UNDER VEST.

BRING LEFT ARM UP THROUGH THE LOOP.

PULL LOOP DOWN FROM UNDER VEST.

THUMB STILL IN POCKET.

Bring the loop over your helper's head, one side at the back and the other in front. Then bring it down and put it into the neck part of the vest.

Bring the loop over the left shoulder and helper's arm up through it.

Pull the loop down from under the vest and let it drop to the floor. Helper steps out.

This trick may be done with a T shirt, the wearer holding the lower end, which must be outside the trousers.

LOOP AND SCISSORS TRICK

Put the center of a piece of cord

about four feet long up through one of the handle sections of a pair of scissors. The section is marked *A* in the drawing. A small bend or loop will be made. Through this bend and through *B* put both ends of the cord.

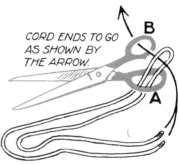

CORD ENDS TO GO AS SHOWN BY THE ARROW.

B

A

The cord and bend should now be as pictured. The ends are to be tied to a chair, a doorknob, or just held by someone until the trick is done. The trick is to get the scissors free from the loop. Let your friends try first.

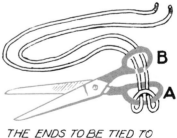

B

A

THE ENDS TO BE TIED TO SOMETHING STEADY OR HELD BY SOMEBODY.

Move the scissors up along the cord and bring the bend up from *A* and put it through *B*. Now bring

95

the bend over the points of the scissors.

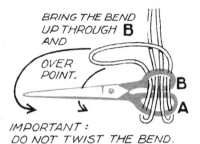

BRING THE BEND
UP THROUGH **B**
AND

OVER
POINT.

B

A

IMPORTANT :
DO NOT TWIST THE BEND.

Bring the bend all the way over the scissors beyond *A* and *B*. You will have no trouble in getting the scissors off the cord.

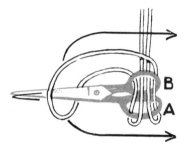

B

A

Practice this trick a few times with the cord ends tied to something steady before you do it in front of an audience. Be sure when bringing the bend over the points of the scissors as shown in picture No. 3, that you do not get a twist in the loop.

DOUBLE-CUT CORD RESTORED

Tie a piece of easily cut cord or string not more than three and a half feet long so as to make a loop. Make

the knot as close as possible to the ends. Have a scissors ready for the cutting.

Hold the loop as shown with the knot just outside the left thumb and first finger. Have the part of the loop on the far side a little bit longer than the part on the near side.

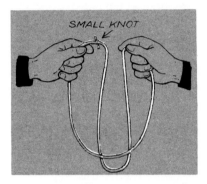

SMALL KNOT

The left hand is to bring the knot around the far side of the string held by the right and take it back again. This time hide the knot under your thumb. Bring your hands together.

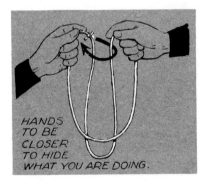

HANDS
TO BE
CLOSER
TO HIDE
WHAT YOU ARE DOING.

Both ends of the loop will now be linked as shown. The hands should be closer with the fingers hiding the linking. The right hand is to take the link from the left just beyond the knot and draw it out about an inch or less.

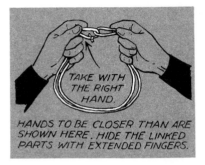

TAKE WITH THE RIGHT HAND.

HANDS TO BE CLOSER THAN ARE SHOWN HERE. HIDE THE LINKED PARTS WITH EXTENDED FINGERS.

The right thumb and first finger now hide the knot. Ask somebody to take the scissors and cut across the parts marked by the arrow. When

CUT

KNOTTED LINK UNDER THUMB

YOUR HELPER IS TO CUT ACROSS BOTH PARTS OF THE STRING

cut, put the right hand part in your mouth and work the knot part off with your tongue.

With your right hand take the string from your mouth, hiding the bend for a moment before pulling it out straight. Keep the knot in your mouth until you get a chance to dispose of it without being seen.

STRING AND STRAW CUT

An eighteen-inch piece of string is put into a soda straw and brought through until the ends of the string hanging out are of equal length. The straw with the string in it is then bent at the center, and cut in half with scissors. The straw halves are pulled off and the string is shown to be in one piece! Use a large-size straw.

Your den chief, who is to know the secret, is to prepare the straw for you by cutting a three-inch slit with a razor blade along the center of the straw. Let your friends see the string being put through the straw.

Bend the straw so that the slit will be on the under side.

Hold as shown, with the back of your hand toward your audience.

First, pull the string ends down with the right hand. The center of the string will come through the slit

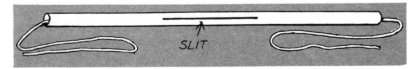

SLIT

SLIT

AUDIENCE TO SEE THE THE TIP OF THE BENT PART.

CENTER OF STRING

PUT LEFT THUMB ON THE CENTER OF THE STRING AND HOLD.

the straw in half. Hold the center of the string with your thumb against your hand. Put the scissors away and with your right hand draw the straw halves off the string. With your right hand pretend to fix the string in your left and then show it.

A SURPRISE CUTTING OF LOOP KNOTS

For the rope tricks shown on these pages you will use a number of different lengths of rope. On a table with these lengths, but separated a little from them so that they can be picked up easily, have three lengths, one of which is four feet long and two of which are two feet long. The two shorter ropes are tied together with a small knot. The four-foot rope is bent at the center and seems to be tied at the bend so that it looks like the two tied ropes. The ropes or cords used should be easy to cut with scissors and should not be kinky. Your audience should be seated at some distance from your table and should not be allowed to crowd around it. Have scissors on the table.

Secretly prepare the ropes before you perform. Bring over the center of the four-foot rope so as to make

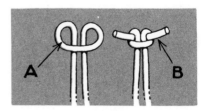

A   B

unseen. Then slide your left hand down a bit to leave enough space at the bend for the blade of a scissors to go through for the cutting. Cut

98

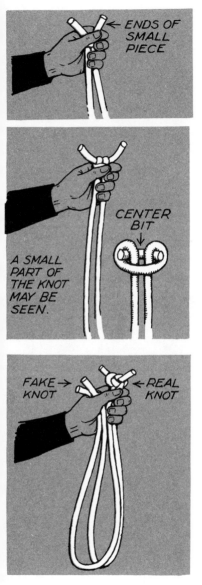

ENDS OF SMALL PIECE

CENTER BIT

A SMALL PART OF THE KNOT MAY BE SEEN.

FAKE→ KNOT ←REAL KNOT

two small loops. The loops are marked *A* in the drawing. Through the loops put a four-inch bit of rope,

marked as *B*. Tighten the loops to get what looks like a knot.

Hold fake knot as shown when you pick up the rope.

EXTRA KNOTS TO BE MADE BY AUDIENCE

Pick up the tied short ropes and take them to your audience. Ask some person to tie the loose ends so as to make a loop.

This person is to stand up and show the loop which he is to hold until the cutting. Give the scissors to a second person.

Go back to the table, pick up the faked rope and hold it so that only the ends of the four-inch bit of rope can be seen. Take the rope to a third person and, as you hold the hidden fake knot, have him tie the free ends together.

Take the loop from this person with your free hand and hold the knot just made the same way you are holding the fake knot. Show the loop to all.

The four knots are now to be cut. Have some grown-up person cut the two knots of the loop held in the audience. He or she may be the person who tied its loose ends. The person who cuts should stand facing the audience.

Tell him or her to cut off the loose ends of the knots or cut through small parts so as to open the knots and separate the two ropes. Thank this person for helping you, and then let the real knot end of the loop you are holding drop. With your free hand take the scissors. You may say that you are going to show how a magician cuts knots.

With the hand holding the scissors, bring up the real knot and put it in the other hand just above the thumb and first finger. When doing this, push the fake knot in between the thumb and first finger, as shown, leaving only the ends of the fake to be seen.

The back of the hand holding the knots is to be on the audience side.

The drawing shows your view of hand and knots.

Start by cutting off the ends of the real knot. You may have to cut a part of the knot to open it. Let the free ends drop. Now, cut the partly-hidden fake knot.

Snip off the ends. With the scissors pick out the small center bit and pretend to cut it. Let it drop. Still hiding the fake knot, bring up the free ends and take one in each hand. Suddenly pull the rope out straight.

SURPRISE SEPARATION OF TIED ROPES

Two pieces of rope each four feet long are knotted together by two helpers. While they hold the ends you can separate the ropes although they stay knotted.

Practice doing this trick with two friends until you are sure that you can do it well before an audience. When you are about to do the trick say that you need two helpers.

Of course, one or both of your friends with whom you have been practicing may come up, but if you are sure you can perform the trick, any two helpers will do.

Link the ropes as shown here, marked A and B. Take either of the two ends and hold them up in one hand. This is to let your audience see without having to be told that the ropes are linked. Suppose you hold up A in your left hand and the B ends are hanging down.

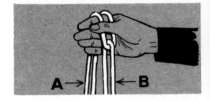

With your right hand take hold of the A parts just above the bend where A and B are linked.

With your left hand bring the A parts down at the back of your right. Let them hang with the B parts. Now invite two people to come and tie the two ropes together.

While your helpers are coming forward, take hold of A with both hands close to where B is hanging across A's center as shown here. Have one helper stand at your right side and the other at your left. You are to stand facing the audience. Your helpers may stand sideways to the audience.

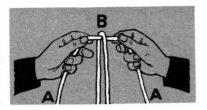

While talking to your helpers get the right-hand part of *A* with your right middle or other fingers in between the hanging parts of *B*. Bring both parts of *A* together with your left fingers. Take both parts of *B* with your right fingers.

Practice these moves without looking at your hands.

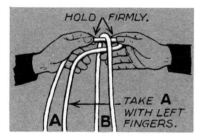

HOLD FIRMLY.

TAKE **A** WITH LEFT FINGERS.

The ropes now should be as shown. Hold the half-inch bend of *A* for a moment with your right thumb and first finger until left thumb and finger take and hold both bends. Let a small bit of *A* be

seen. Slide right hand along the *B* parts and give the ends to the helpers at your right to tie a knot close to the bend.

The knots shown here are drawn more open than they should be so that you can see what they are like. Your left thumb and fingers have been holding the bends for the first knot. Cover left hand with the right; slide left out and get a grip on the bends with right thumb and fingers. Give the *A* ends to the helper at your left who is to tie the second knot. Hold the bends tight.

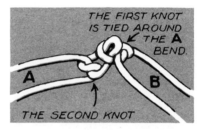

THE FIRST KNOT IS TIED AROUND THE **A** BEND.

A   **B**

THE SECOND KNOT

Take the rope ends from your helpers and, holding the knots, let all four ends drop. With your free hand take an *A* and a *B* end and hold them up. Show the knots for a moment. Cover them again and give each helper an *A* end and a *B* end to hold. Each hand is to hold

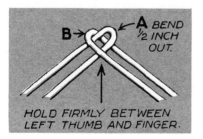

A BEND ½ INCH OUT.

B →

HOLD FIRMLY BETWEEN LEFT THUMB AND FINGER.

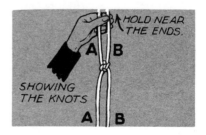

HOLD NEAR THE ENDS.

A **B**

SHOWING THE KNOTS

A **B**

one end only. Under cover of your hands push the *A* bend out of the *B* knot. The ropes with knots will be separated.

STRINGING A FRIEND

Cut in half a piece of white twisted string or cord six feet long. Cut one of the halves in half. The string should be the soft heavy kind used for tying packages.

Take the long string and open it at the center as shown. The opening must be not less than two inches in length and the sides *A* and *B* of equal thickness. Pull sides out.

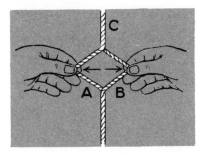

Twist *A* and *B* and bring them up. Bring *C* down. When showing, hold part *D* between thumb and

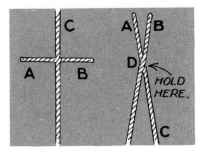

fingers. What you hold will look like two separate pieces of string.

Put the fixed piece and one of the others into one hand as shown. Then add what seems to be the fourth piece. Now give your friend the two short pieces.

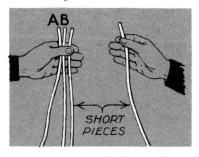

Tell your friend to do the same as you do. Take up one of the hanging ends and let it down at the back of your hand. Close the hand on the string and pull fixed part down into it.

When ready, tell your friend to take hold of one of the long ends and pull the string out. Wait until he does this. He will be holding two pieces. When you pull an end slide your hand off the fixed part to the other end and pull hard. You will be holding a long single string.

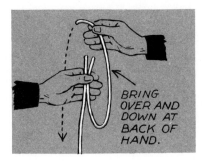

STRINGING AN AUDIENCE

In your audience have a secret helper who ought to be in the first or second row. Have three pairs of eighteen-inch strings and add them to the fixed piece that you first put into your hand as described in the "stringing a friend" trick. Go to your audience and give pairs of strings to different people who must not be seated near each other. One of these people may be your helper. Go back to your place and do the trick the same way as you did it with one person. When all have failed to join the pieces and you have shown yours "joined," somebody may hold up two strings and ask you to join them. Your helper may do this if nobody else does. Put your string aside and collect the six short strings. Say that you will put them all together. Hold up the ball and say, "Now they are all together." Wait a moment and then say, "But I guess you want to make them into one string." Say, "I need a rubber band. Has anybody got one?" Your helper is to rise and say,

"I think I have one." He is to search his pockets in one of which he has a band and in another a small ball of string, nine feet long, with a rubber band wrapped around it.

With one hand he is to show the band and keep the other hand closed on his lap. This hand is to hide the ball. Give him your ball and tell him to wrap the rubber band around it. With practice he should be able to do this easily, using the first finger and thumb of the hand hiding the prepared ball. When the band is on your ball, your helper is to push it into his free hand and with the first finger of this hand get hold of the prepared ball in the other hand and give it to you.

While you hold up the ball for all to see, your helper can put the ball you gave him in his pocket. Go to your place, make a magic sign over the ball, and take the rubber band off. Pull out the string bit by bit. When you have pulled out a small piece ask somebody to hold it. Keep unwinding the ball until you are holding the other end of the long string.

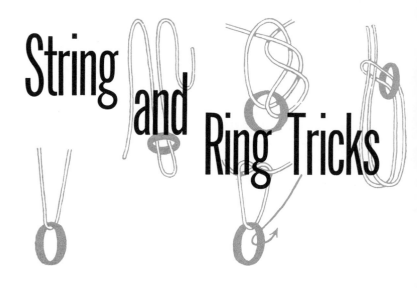

String and Ring Tricks

THE STRINGS to be used in the following tricks should be white so that they can be seen easily at a distance. They must not be kinky. If there are kinks you can get rid of them by pulling your string backwards and forwards a few times over the edge of a board or table. Press hard on the string as you pull.

The string ought to be the strong kind used in tying big packages. It should not be less than a sixteenth of an inch in thickness. Cut several pieces each two feet long.

The rings will not all be the same kind. They will differ according to the trick. Magicians often borrow a ring from some person in the audience, but it is better that you have your own. Get a plain finger ring at a dime store. A metal washer may be

used, but only when you cannot get a real ring.

For two of the tricks, candy and cardboard rings are to be used. For one trick you will need two plain bracelets such as are sold at dime stores.

TO GET A RING OFF A STRING OF MANY KNOTS (FIRST METHOD)

Bend the string at its center. Put the bend a little way through the ring.

Bring both ends of the string over the ring and put them through the bend as shown.

Pull the string ends all the way through the bend until you get what looks like a knot.

To free the ring spread the bend

as shown by *A* and then down as shown by *B*. Arrows show the way.

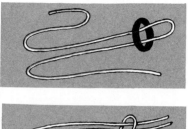

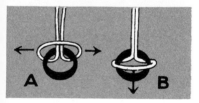

FAKE KNOT EASILY SLIPPED OFF.

Doing the Trick

On a table not too close to your audience have your secretly prepared string with the knot. Cover this string more or less with other pieces of string. Pick up one of these pieces and say that you are going to tie a ring on it but that you would like to have somebody help you tie a lot of knots as well. Put the string down close to the one with the ring and while your helper is coming forward, get the prepared string and pretend that you are just tying the ring on it. Tie a couple of real knots about half an inch above the fake one. Take up the string ends and swing the ring a little bit. Cover the fake knot and the half inch of string above it with your thumb and fingers. Give the string ends to your helper to tie as many knots as he wishes. When he has tied them cover his hands holding the string, all of the knots, and the ring with a handkerchief. Put both hands under the handkerchief and remove the ring as shown. Take the handkerchief away and show the freed ring.

TO GET A RING OFF A STRING WITH MANY KNOTS (SECOND METHOD)

The knot in this trick is not secretly prepared as it is in the first method. Your audience sees you tying it and also sees you making the knot look as though it would be hard to untie. When you have made the knot and the extra string twists, ask some person to come and tie more knots.

Tie a single knot with *A* and *B* over the ring, at the center of the string.

Bring *A* down and put it through the ring from your side.

Put the *A* end through the knot loop from your side. Pull *A* and *B*.

When *A* and *B* are pulled you will get this fake knot.

Taking the Ring Off

When pulling to get the fake knot, hide the knot and ring in one hand. When you have the fake, tie a couple of knots about half an inch above it as your helper is coming forward to tie more knots. Finish the trick as described in the first method.

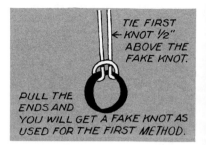

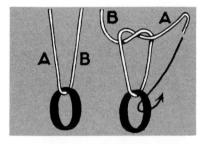

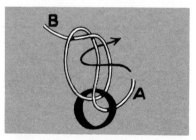

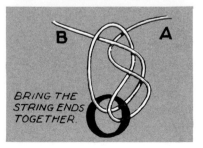

TAKING A RING OFF A TWICE-KNOTTED STRING

This trick will need lots of practice so that you will be able to do the first part easily and quickly. This first part of the trick gets the ring out of the knots before you take it off the string.

You may have a friend hold the string ends while you practice, or you may tie the ends to the back of a chair or to drawer handles if you want to practice secretly. After some practice, try to free the ring just by feeling instead of looking at what you are doing.

Bring the ring to the center of the string. Tie two loose knots. The two loops made are to be bigger than the ring. Although your string will be white, one half is shown as black in the drawing to help you in making the moves.

Suppose you select the black half marked as *B*. Bring the ring up along it, over and under the white *A* half, the way the *B* half goes until it is outside the knots, and up along *B*.

Before making these moves let

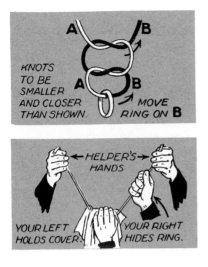

KNOTS TO BE SMALLER AND CLOSER THAN SHOWN.

A B

MOVE RING ON **B**

←HELPER'S→ HANDS

YOUR LEFT HOLDS COVER.

YOUR RIGHT HIDES RING.

your audience see you making the knots.

Invite some person to come and hold the string ends, one end in each hand.

Put a handkerchief between *A* and *B* to cover the knots and the ring before you make the moves. When both hands have freed the ring, hold the handkerchief over the knots with your left hand. Hide the ring in your right hand and slide this hand up along *B* until it is close to your helper's left hand.

Say to him, "I want you to hold the string this way." Move his hand off the end of the string. Stretch the string out and let him take it again between your hand and the handkerchief. Slide your hand off and put it under the handkerchief, which your left lifts to show the freed ring.

THE RING PUT BACK

Two rings, exactly alike, are needed for this trick planned to follow the one just described.

First, give the ring you removed during the preceding trick to someone for examination. Your helper is to untie the two loose knots, as the ring is being examined. The second ring is hidden in your helper's right hand, under his third and little fingers. He should hide it there before he comes to help you with the first trick. He should keep it hidden until he unties the knots and then secretly puts a string through it. Draw the string halfway through and let the ends drop.

Hold your ring up between your right thumb and first finger with the handkerchief in the other three fingers. Look at your helper and tell him that he has to tie the knots again. Put your left hand under his right, hiding his ring. Keeping the ring hidden, take it with the string.

As your helper holds the ends of the tied string, cover your left hand with the handkerchief.

Take your left hand out and put your right, with its ring, underneath.

Wait a few seconds and then put your left fingers on top of the handkerchief and through it get hold of the right hand ring.

Take away the handkerchief and extra ring and pocket them. Point to the other ring with your right hand. To make this trick completely effective, be sure the audience does not see the extra ring. Practice methods of concealing it before you do the trick.

TAKING A RING OFF A LOOPED STRING

Tie a string two feet long to make a loop. Put one of the loop ends through a ring and bring the ring to the center of the loop as shown. Ask a friend to hold up his first fingers; put a loop end over each finger. Have the knot on your side of the loop and near your helper's left finger. Tell him you will take off the ring without taking the loop off his fingers.

So that you can see what is to be done, your hands are not shown in this picture. Halfway between the ring and your helper's left finger, put a hand over the loop and pick up the string part that is on the far side. Bring this part as a bend down over your helper's right finger and the loop end as well.

The bend brought over must go outside the loop end on the finger. Slip this end off and the ring will be freed. The loop will be left on both fingers.

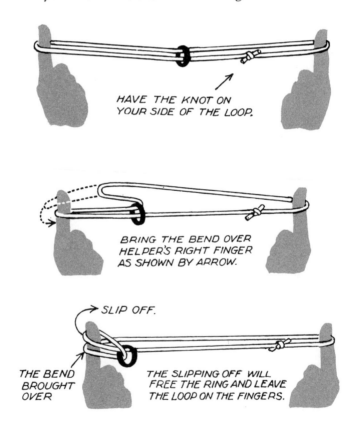

HAVE THE KNOT ON
YOUR SIDE OF THE LOOP.

BRING THE BEND OVER
HELPER'S RIGHT FINGER
AS SHOWN BY ARROW.

SLIP OFF.

THE BEND
BROUGHT
OVER

THE SLIPPING OFF WILL
FREE THE RING AND LEAVE
THE LOOP ON THE FINGERS.

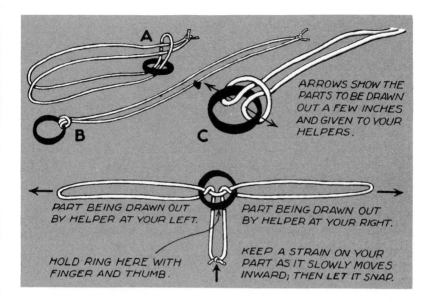

ARROWS SHOW THE PARTS TO BE DRAWN OUT A FEW INCHES AND GIVEN TO YOUR HELPERS.

PART BEING DRAWN OUT BY HELPER AT YOUR LEFT.

PART BEING DRAWN OUT BY HELPER AT YOUR RIGHT.

HOLD RING HERE WITH FINGER AND THUMB.

KEEP A STRAIN ON YOUR PART AS IT SLOWLY MOVES INWARD; THEN LET IT SNAP.

TO TAKE A RING OFF A LOOP HELD BY THREE PEOPLE

Tie your string to make a loop. Stretch the loop and put one end through a ring. Through this end put the other end as shown by *A*. Pull this tied end all the way through as shown by *B*. Hold up the loop by the tied end and swing the ring a little bit as you invite two people to help you do the trick. While your helpers are coming, loosen the two parts of the string marked by the arrows and pull them out a small way from the inside of the ring as shown by *C*. Your helpers are to stand slightly in front of you, one at each side. Give one of the small pulled-out parts to one helper and one to the other helper. You are to hold the tied end. Take hold of the ring on your side with a thumb and

finger. Say that you are going to try to take the ring off while the string is being held.

Tell your helpers to pull steadily. Keep a good grip on your end as it is being pulled toward the ring. Make it look as though you also were pulling outward. Suddenly let your end go and say "Off!" To your helper's and everybody's surprise, show the freed ring held between your thumb and finger.

STRING AND MANY RINGS

For this trick the rings are to be the colored hard-candy rings that come wrapped in rolls. There are eleven candies in a roll, so you will need two rolls. You will also need a white string two feet long and a tin coffee can with its cover. Have a large handkerchief in your breast pocket.

Place the can and cover on a chair or table. The cover is to be a tray on which you pile the candies. A red candy is secretly prepared and is to be separated a little from the others.

To prepare the red candy, put a knife across it and give the knife a sharp tap. The candy will split in half. Lick the four ends and put the halves together. You will have a ring that can be broken easily. This ring is to be the first to go on the string. The last ring to go on must be red also.

When the red candy is prepared, let the halves stay stuck together for a while. Then try breaking them apart with your fingers. You may find that the joined parts have hardened too much to break easily. Separate them, lick the ends, and put the halves together again. This will help soften the ends.

Do not have the ring joined too long before you do the trick because the joined parts might harden too much.

Put both string ends together through the next ring which may be any color except red. Let this ring drop down along the doubled string. When a few rings have been put on, stop and say that the red candy is there as a stop light to hold the others for a while. Continue to put the rings on until you come to the last one which must be red. Say nothing about this candy.

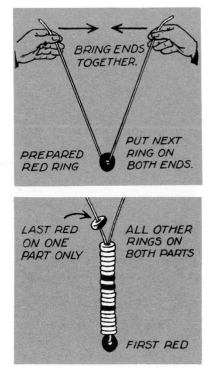

Under cover of your fingers put the last ring on one string end only. Keep it and a few other rings covered as you ask somebody to come and hold the string ends. They are to be held with one hand. Your helper is to hold the can with his other hand. Quickly cover the candies and the hand holding the string with your handkerchief.

Taking All Rings Off Except One

Have your helper standing slightly sideways to your audience. He is to hold the can low under the candies and hold the string up so that you can easily put your hands under

110

the handkerchief without touching the can.

Say that you are going to turn off the red stop light for a couple of seconds. Put both hands under the handkerchief and break the red candy. Let it and all of the candies rattle down into the coffee can. The last red will drop to the center of the string where the first one was. You may say, "Red light on again." Take the handkerchief away and let the red candy be seen. Take the string and the can from your helper and put them on the table or chair. Thank your helper and give him some of the candies. Pick out the broken halves and put them in your mouth. You may also give your helper the can and ask him to share the candies in it with people in the audience.

CARDBOARD RINGS AND STRING

The rings for this trick are holes punched in small cards cut from thin, easily torn cardboard. The cards are to be two inches long by one and a half inches wide. The hole in each card is to be punched near one of the ends as shown on the next page. You will need at least twelve cards, and they are to be of three or four different colors.

Packages of sheets of this thin cardboard or thick paper may be purchased at most dime stores. Have your den chief or Den Mother make enough of these cards for you so that you will have extra ones for practice. Except for the last part, the trick is done the same way as you do the trick with the candy rings.

Put a red card on the string, then double the string and put on the other cards, mixing the colors. The last card, a red one, is to go on one string end only. Slide it down and cover it and a few of the others with your hand. Ask someone to hold the string ends. Cover his hand and the cards with a handkerchief.

THE FIRST CARD,
A RED ONE, TO BE
AT THE CENTER
OF THE STRING.

BRING THE STRING
ENDS TOGETHER FOR
2" THE OTHER CARDS.
LAST, A RED, ON ONE OF
THE ENDS.

← 1½" →

Put your hands under and tear the bottom card off at the hole. Crumple this card into a small wad and keep it hidden in one hand. The cards may not fall off like the candies did, and you may have to pull them off with your hands. Let them drop on the floor. Bring the last card to the center of the string. Stand so that your hand with the crumpled card is away from the audience. With your free hand take off the handkerchief. Ask your helper to examine the card on the string. While he is doing this put the wad of cardboard in your trouser pocket.

PUTTING A BIG RING ON A STRING TIED TO YOUR WRISTS

To do this trick you must be wearing a coat with fairly loose sleeves. The coat should not be buttoned. With your string you will need two big rings. Get two plain bracelets at a dime store. They must be exactly alike in size and color. The best kind are the plastic ones that come in many bright colors.

Secretly, before you perform, one of these rings must be put on your left arm and pushed up your sleeve until it is near your elbow.

Keep this arm bent so that the ring will not slip down and be seen. Hold the string in one hand and the second ring in the other. Ask some person to tie the string ends fairly tight around your wrists. While he is doing the tying keep your hands higher than your elbows. Let him examine the ring to see that there are no breaks or openings in it.

With your left hand take the ring from your helper and show it. Say that you will try to get it on the string. Turn your back to your help-

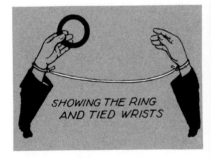

SHOWING THE RING
AND TIED WRISTS

SHOWING THE RING MAGICALLY ON THE STRING

er and the audience. Bring your hands together and with your right open the right side of your coat a little bit. With your left, quickly put the ring it is holding into your inside coat pocket.

Bring both hands down and let the ring hidden on your arm slide down over your left hand and onto the string. You may have to use your right hand to get the ring down and to the center of the string. All these moves should take but a few seconds. Turn around and show the ring on the string. Thank your helper and have him untie the knots.

MAGNETIC PENCILS AND RING

Have two new pencils in your breast pocket, eraser ends up. Dark-colored pencils are best for the trick.

Tie a small knot as close as you can to one end of a fifteen-inch piece of black thread. Insert the knotted end into a slit in the eraser of the pencil on the left. The knot will keep the thread from being pulled out. Tie the other end of the thread

to a middle button of your shirt.

Take both pencils out of your pocket with your left hand, keeping the eraser ends up. With your right hand, take the pencil without the thread away from the other as far as possible. Be careful not to get the pencil caught in the thread. Say that you will rub the pencils together to make them magnetic. Hold the one with the thread upright, about eight inches from your chest. Rub the other pencil crosswise and up and down against the threaded pencil. Put the free pencil down on a table or chair where you have a ring.

Holding the threaded pencil at the lower end, drop the ring over the pencil and the thread. Let the ring slide down and rest on your fingers. Now, take the other pencil; hold it level; and put it under the thread. As you slowly raise the pencil, the ring will move upward.

When near the top, let the ring drop down about halfway. Repeat, making the ring go up and down a few times.

Complete the trick with a quick, high lift of the free pencil, causing the ring to shoot off the pencil and thread.

The quick lift may break the thread or pull it out of the slit. Nobody will notice it if you pull the thread forward and out of the slit with your right hand.

Handkerchief, Neckerchief, and Napkin Tricks

A NUMBER of tricks described on the following pages have to do with knots, some being done in almost the same way as the knot tricks with rope. However, to your audience they will look very different. Some of the handkerchief tricks will need a lot of practice, and this means that your handkerchief will get a lot of crumpling and will not stay clean enough for use in your show.

When performing, use handkerchiefs that have not been starched but have been ironed. For most of the tricks white linen or cotton handkerchiefs will be all right, and for some tricks colored ones may be used.

Do not use handkerchiefs with colored patterns or designs on them.

Two of the following tricks are done with Cub Scout neckerchiefs and one with paper napkins. These paper napkins should be the heavy paper kind that you cannot see through, and they should have straight edges.

FAST KNOT

Hold a handkerchief near a corner with the left hand. Take and slide the right hand toward the opposite corner.

Turn right hand under, inward, and up, as shown by the arrow. Now show the handkerchief for a few seconds. Make the next moves as quickly as you can. Practice slowly.

Separate the first and second fingers of each hand. Bring your hands together with your left on the inside. With left fingers take hold of B and with the right take A as shown by the arrows. Separate your hands quickly and you will have a knot.

Do not stop, but throw the handkerchief in the air, catch it, and show the knot.

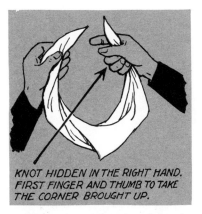

KNOT HIDDEN IN THE RIGHT HAND.
FIRST FINGER AND THUMB TO TAKE
THE CORNER BROUGHT UP.

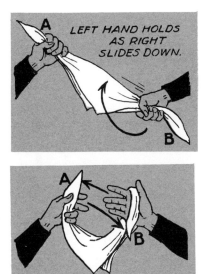

LEFT HAND HOLDS
AS RIGHT
SLIDES DOWN.

A

B

A

B

TAKE CLOSER IN FROM THE
ENDS THAN IS SHOWN HERE.

Hold the knotted end and let the rest drop down. Point to the lowest corner with your left hand and say that sometimes you are able to throw a knot on it. Your act is to try a couple of times and fail. On the third try you make the knot.

Lift the lower corner with your left hand and put it in between your right first finger and thumb with the knot corner already there.

Holding the knot corner tight, snap out the other corner. Say, "Missed it that time."

For the third try, secretly switch the corners. Grip the corner without the knot and snap out the corner with the knot.

THROWING A KNOT

Have a knot already made near a corner of your handkerchief. Put the handkerchief in your pocket so that when taking it out you will be able to hide the knot in your hand. Take it out with your right hand.

THE VANISHING KNOT

A handkerchief slightly rolled is to be held near one corner between the first and second fingers of the left hand at A as shown on next page. Right hand to hold B.

Put corner B across the left first

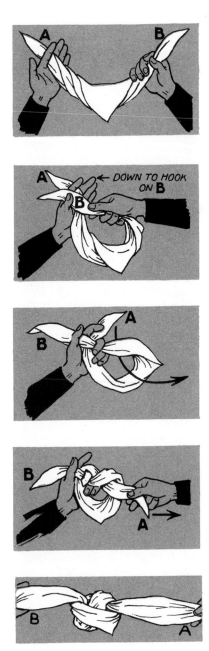

finger. Close your left thumb on *B* to hold it.

Bring left second finger down to get a hook grip on *B* also.

Left second finger grips *B* and is helped by third finger. Thumb also holds it. Put your right hand through the loop and take *A*. Pull *A* through the loop.

As the right hand pulls *A*, your left second finger hooked on *B* is to pull *B* part way back through the loop. Your third left finger is to help the hooked second.

Pull *A* until the knot is tight and then stop. Take your second left finger out of the bend and holding either or both corners of the handkerchief, show the knot. It is really a slipknot ready to come apart. Holding corners *B* and *A*, bring the knot a few inches from your mouth. Blow quickly on the knot and at the same moment jerk lightly on the corners. Do not jerk too hard because your audience is to think that you just blew the knot away.

RABBIT FROM A HANDKERCHIEF

Tell your friends that magicians usually pull rabbits out of hats, but you will show them that you can get a rabbit from a handkerchief. Let them see you make it.

Put a handkerchief on your right arm so that the side edges hang even. The edge at *C* is to be two inches beyond your fingers.

With your left hand put *C* in under and hold it with your right

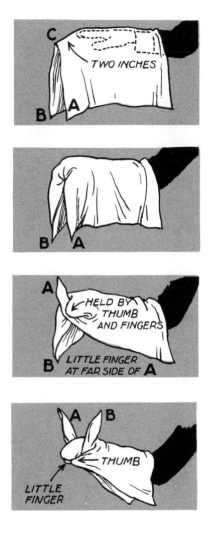

TWO INCHES

C

B A

B A

A
HELD BY
THUMB
AND FINGERS

B LITTLE FINGER
AT FAR SIDE OF A

A B

THUMB

LITTLE
FINGER

SHOWING THE RABBIT

Bring corner *B* over and put it between your thumb and first finger. Pull it up to make the second ear. Bring your thumb and little finger under the other fingers.

Hold the rabbit against your chest and put your left arm around it. Give it a couple of pats and then make it jump up a few times toward your left shoulder. If you wish, have a small carrot in your pocket. Take it out and put it in your rabbit's mouth, which is between your thumb and fingers. Let him chew on one of your left fingers.

HANDKERCHIEF PUPPET NO. 1

Tie a knot in a corner of your handkerchief and put your right first finger into it. If you are left-handed put your left first finger in the knot. Bring the hanging parts around each side of your hand from the back and cross them in front.

thumb and fingers. Your little finger is not to do any holding.

Bring corner *A* across in front and under the fingers and put it in between your little and third fingers. Pull the corner up to make one of the rabbit's ears.

117

Hold these parts with your third and little fingers. Stick your thumb and second finger up to be the hands as shown. The knot makes the puppet's head.

Lots of funny movements can be made, such as beating time to music, nodding the head, bringing the head down between the hands to be scratched, pointing at a person or something that you may be talking about.

For shadow fun make a puppet for your other hand. You will need a good strong light and a flat white surface as a screen for the shadows.

When showing, sit below the screen so that your own shadow will not be on it and so that your audience will have a clear view.

Give one of the puppets a short pencil to hold. On the screen it will look like a big stick.

The puppet shadows will look like two old ladies, and they are supposed to be having an argument.

Nod their heads one at a time, not too fast at first. Move the hands, and after a while have the one hold-

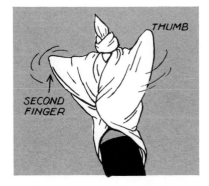

ing the pencil hit the other one a few times.

The injured one ends your show by reaching over, grabbing the end of the knot, and pulling the head off the puppet with the stick.

HANDKERCHIEF PUPPET NO. 2

Tie a knot at the center of handkerchief edge. Tie a big one first and then slide it up to be a small one. Next tie the corners of the edge *A* and *B* together to make the puppet's arms. Roll the *C* and *D* edge up to the arms and then tie the *C* and *D* corners together. Your puppet will look like the one in the second picture. As he is a handkerchief, let us call him Hank.

Hank, the Dancer

Hank is to dance on a stage or platform, and you will need a helper. A few things have to be prepared secretly. Your Den Mother or den chief can be your helper in the preparations and also in the dancing. A screw or eye hook is to be fixed in the ceiling or high up over

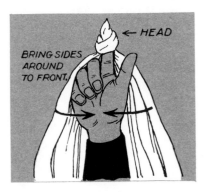

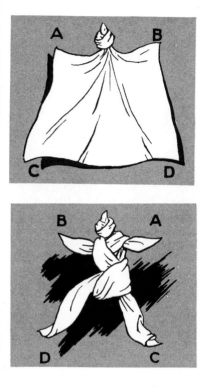

that he loves to dance. Put him on the floor. If there is a piano, ask for music. Your helper is to pull just enough to make Hank sit up for a moment and then get up on his feet. While dancing, Hank is not to be pulled too high off the floor at any time.

The thread will not be seen, especially if the stage is not too brightly lighted and you have a flashlight shining on Hank.

At the end, untie Hank's knots and show the handkerchief. While opening the handkerchief, break the thread or slip it off.

THE EGG LAYER

Spread out and show a handkerchief; fold it in half and hold it over a hat. An egg is seen to drop from the handkerchief into the hat! The handkerchief is spread over the hat and then lifted. You show both sides of the handkerchief, fold it in half, and hold it over the hat as before. Again an egg is seen to drop into the hat. This egg-dropping can be repeated as often as you like, but six times ought to be enough.

For this trick a large red bandanna handkerchief is much better than a white one. You may say that you got it from a farmer who sold chickens and eggs.

Prepare an egg by making a small hole at each end and blowing the insides out through one of the holes. It will help if you give the egg a few good shakes first. Break a

the spot where Hank is to dance. A very long strong black thread is to go through the hook. One end of the thread is to be tied around Hank's neck and the other end held by your helper. Your helper sits behind a folding screen or a screen with an opening in it through which the thread is to go and through which the helper can see. If there is a place at either side of the stage where the helper can be out of sight, the screen will not be needed.

You are to come on with Hank sticking up out of your pocket. Take him out, introduce him, and say

119

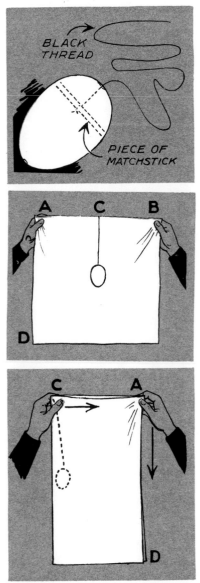

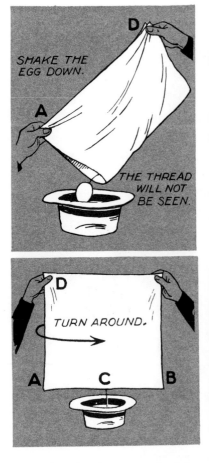

matchstick so that it can fit cross-wise in the shell as shown above. To the center of the match tie a black thread and put an end of the match into the shell. Push the matchstick all the way in. When it is inside pull on the thread so that the match will be caught and can not slip out. Do not pull hard.

Fasten the thread to one of the handkerchief edges at its center so that the egg will hang down to the middle of the handkerchief as shown. This view is your side of the handkerchief when it is being shown to your audience. When showing, do not look at the egg. Before showing, have the handkerchief with the egg under it lying on a table beside a farmer's straw hat or a hat borrowed from some person in the audience. The hat should be upside down and the handkerchief crumpled a bit. The thread edge C should be your side.

Fold corner A over on B. Square the fold at C. Bring your left hand over from C to take A and B. Slide your right hand down to take the two corners at D.

Raise the D corners and bring C a couple of inches over the hat. With your right hand gently shake the egg into the hat. The thread will not be seen.

Keeping the handkerchief over the hat, take the D corners and open the handkerchief. Turn it around so that both sides are shown. Then spread it over the hat, putting the D corners toward the audience and having the A and B corners on your side.

More Eggs

Take up the corners A and B and lift the spread handkerchief to bring up the egg on your side. You will now be ready to repeat the moves. Bring the A and B corners together.

When you have dropped the egg six times, say that you think half a dozen will be enough. Put the handkerchief aside and look into the hat. Count and pretend to touch six eggs. With both hands take the hat brim

and carefully carry the hat to its owner. Turn it over just as you give it to him. If you use the farmer's hat, carry it carefully and then suddenly spin it back to the table.

MENDING A MATCH BY MAGIC

A kitchen match is placed on a handkerchief the corners of which are then folded over to cover the match. People see this being done, and two or three of them are asked to feel the match through the covering to make sure that it is still there.

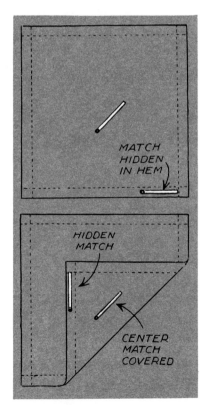

MATCH HIDDEN IN HEM

HIDDEN MATCH

CENTER MATCH COVERED

One person is asked to break it in half and another to break the halves in smaller pieces.

The magician who holds the handkerchief takes a second match and says it is his magic wand and that with it he will mend the broken one. He touches this match to the handkerchief, which he opens to show that the match inside is unbroken.

A handkerchief is secretly prepared by having a match pushed into the hem at one of the corners. This corner with the hidden match is to be sticking up out of your pocket. Taking the corner and holding it with your right thumb and fingers, spread the handkerchief on a table. Have a couple of matches ready on the table. Take one with your left hand and put it on the handkerchief a little off-center in the direction of the corner with the match hidden in the hem.

Take the hidden match corner and bring it over and beyond the match near the center. Next fold in the other three corners bringing all beyond the center of the handkerchief and hold it with both hands. Have your fingertips and thumbs near the ends of the match to be broken which is the one in the hem. Your hands are to cover where the other match is. When unfolding the handkerchief to show the mended match, take the prepared corner with your thumb and fingers to hide it. Shake out the handkerchief and put it in your pocket.

THE NECKERCHIEF PUZZLE

For this trick you will need two straight sticks. They must be smooth and round. One stick is to be ten or twelve inches longer than the other. The long stick may be a cane, a length of broom handle, or a dowel stick. The second stick is to be not more than two feet in length.

TIE ENDS TOGETHER.

You will also need two helpers. They are to hold the long stick, one at each end. One helper is to hold the short stick down at his side. You are to stand behind the long stick as you face the audience.

First hold the ends of the neckerchief and swing it around to get a few twists in it. Then put it around the stick as shown.

Take the short stick from your helper and put it on top of the neckerchief. Your helpers are to hold the ends of this stick also.

Bring end *A* up your side of the short stick and *B* up the other side. Using both hands, bring the ends up at the same time. Next bring them down over the short stick as shown by the arrows.

Bring *A* up your side of both sticks and *B* up at the far side. Now bring the ends together and tie them to each other. Take the short stick from your helpers and draw it out of the neckerchief.

Freeing the Neckerchief

Hold the short stick over the neckerchief that seems to be wrapped around the long stick several times. Say that the short stick is your magic wand and that by just touching the neckerchief with it you will make the neckerchief come free. Touch and then take hold of the knot. Lift it and the neckerchief will be freed. Not as difficult as it seems, the trick should take only a couple of minutes. You may ask others to try it.

NECKERCHIEF THROUGH YOUR LEG

This is a good trick to follow the one with the sticks. If you wish, your den chief or Den Mother can be in on the secret preparations and can tie the knot and dare you to get the neckerchief off. You are to sit forward on a chair or bench so as to have a space back of your legs. You are to be facing your audience.

The neckerchief is to be held by the ends, swung around to get a twist, and then put in front of your knee.

The ends are to be brought back at each side of your leg, the secret "fix" made, and then the ends brought to the front and tied.

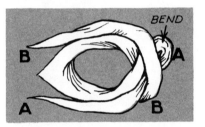

This shows the secret. When the parts of the neckerchief are brought behind your leg, a bend is made in one of them. Either part will do. The other part is to be brought around the bend. As shown here, the bend is made in the *A* part with the *B* part around it. When the "fix" is made, bring your foot back so that your leg will get a good grip on the fixed parts.

Pulling Off

The neckerchief will not come off as long as your leg grips it. Have

123

the short stick used in the other neckerchief trick nearby so that you can easily get it without unbending your leg. If you have a helper, let him or her hold the stick for you.

Grasp the knot and give several hard tugs. Wait a moment and then say that you need your magic wand.

Still holding the knot, take the stick and give the neckerchief a few taps. As you give the last tap, unbend your leg just enough to let you yank the tied neckerchief free.

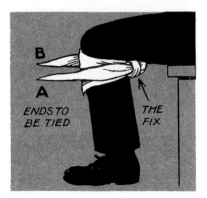

WHERE IS JOE?

Three square paper napkins are to be used. They are to be exactly the same size and must have straight edges. The napkins should be white and made of heavy paper. With a blue or red pencil write or print *Joe* in the center of one of the napkins. Write it again in the center of the other side.

Place Joe on a table so that one of the corners points your way. On top of Joe place the other two napkins each about one inch beyond the other.

Your friends are to see you do it.

Take the near corner of Joe and roll him and the others loosely toward the far corner until two of the bottom far corners flip over. Joe will be the first. The next will cover him. Ask "Where is Joe, top or bottom?"

Your friends will say that Joe is at the bottom. Unroll the napkins and lift off the top one. Joe will be the second one! Arrange the napkins as before, but with Joe as the second one. Roll up again and this time let all three corners flip over. Unroll the napkins and Joe will still be between the other two. With Joe in the middle, roll up again, but let two corners flip this time. Ask "Where is Joe?" "In the middle" will be the answer. Unroll and Joe will be found on the top. Leave him on top when you set the napkins up again. Roll the napkins once more and let two corners flip. Ask again where Joe is. When unrolled, Joe will be found at the bottom.

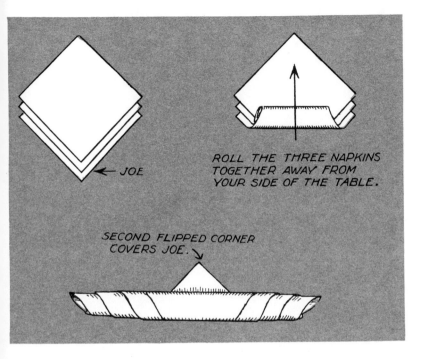

← JOE

ROLL THE THREE NAPKINS
TOGETHER AWAY FROM
YOUR SIDE OF THE TABLE.

SECOND FLIPPED CORNER
COVERS JOE.

Fun with Paper

FOR the tricks shown on the following pages use large double-
page newspaper spreads.

These sheets usually measure
about thirty inches from side to side
and twenty-two and a half inches
from top to bottom.

For cut-out or tear-out designs
like wheels and stars, use sheets
without pictures if you can get them.
If your local papers have pictures
on every page, your den chief or
Den Mother may be able to get
sheets or yards of plain white paper
from the printer. Sheets of thin,
easily torn white wrapping paper
may be used if you cannot get the
newspapers.

Dotted lines on the drawings
show where the folds are made or
where you cut or tear.

There are also letters and inch
marks on the drawings to help when
marking lines to fold and cut.

Your den chief or Den Mother
may have to help you the first few
times with the folding and marking,
but after doing the tricks a few
times, you ought to be able to fold
and cut or tear, without any marks
on the paper.

When you have done your paper
tricks, always be sure to pick up the
torn bits and have something to put
them in.

THE TREE

Make a tube by rolling a double-
page sheet of newspaper from one
side to the other. When about five

126

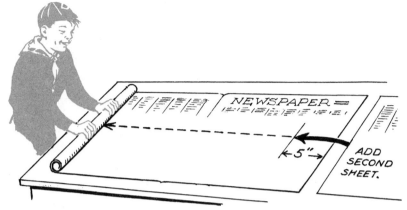

ADD
SECOND
SHEET.

inches from the edge, add another double-page sheet. Keep on rolling and add a third sheet. Bring the paper toward you as you roll it. Tap the ends to keep the roll even.

When the tube is made, your fingers and thumbs should just meet around it. You will have to find out whether or not your fingers are strong enough to tear a tube made of three sheets. At first you may find that you can tear a one-sheet tube only.

Flatten half of the tube and tear straight down the center.

To keep tearing straight, tear about an inch at a time.

Flatten the torn strips together and tear down again.

You may need a clip at the end, but only while tearing.

You will now have four torn parts. Each of the parts will be a lot of strips. Separate the four parts and bend the strips out from the tube. Remove the clip if you used one.

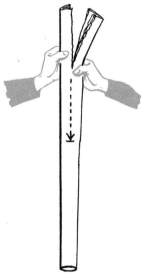

Put two fingers into the tube at the top and with your thumb take hold of a couple of strips where they bend and pull them up gently for a few inches. All strips will start coming up as the tree begins to grow. Take your fingers out at the top and work the tree upwards from the outside.

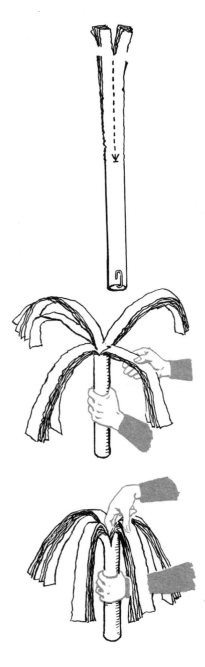

If someone wants to take the tree home, push strips back down as shown at left.

SPREADING THE NEWS

Take a double-page sheet, as used in the tree with the pages together. Roll them down from top to bottom to make a tube with the fold of the paper at one end and the side edges of the pages at the other end.

Flatten the tube in order to get the bottom edges of the pages in line with an edge of the tube.

Try to get the top edge of the paper, now inside the tube, in line with the edge of the tube. The flat tube should be at least three-inches wide.

Tear down the center from the fold to about one inch from the other end. Flatten the tube again in order to get the torn parts on each side. Now, tear the new center up to an inch and one half from the fold end.

Next, separate the bottom edge strip from the others, except for the top edge inside strip if it is in line with the outside one. Bunch the rest and tear all ends off close to the fold. To "spread the news," get friends to help open a big paper chain, formed by the torn newspaper.

THE LATTICE

Tear a flattened tube halfway across and then toward each end as shown here by the dotted lines. When torn, flatten the ends and strips so that the ends can be bent back. Bend the torn parts out and keep the ends flat. Take the ends together in one hand and with the other hand, work the paper out as you did for the tree.

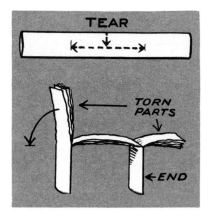

THE LADDER

As shown on the next page, roll the double-page newspaper sheets to make a tube the same way you made the tube for the tree. Use paste or rubber cement along the last side edge of the paper to keep the tube from unrolling.

Flatten the tube and tear it across three quarters of the way at about seven inches from one end. Continue tearing along the tube to about seven inches from the other end and then over to the side from which you started. The dotted lines show where the tube is to be torn. Tear the corners square.

When the center part is torn out, flatten the ends and strips again so that they will be as in the second picture on page 130. Bend the tube ends down and make them round again. Bring the ends together and hold them tightly in one hand.

You are now ready to show your paper ladder. Follow diagrams on next page.

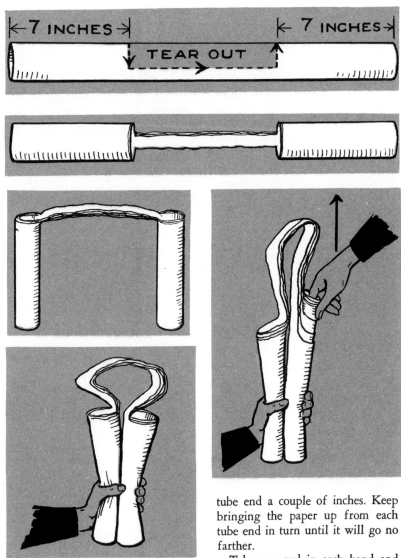

tube end a couple of inches. Keep bringing the paper up from each tube end in turn until it will go no farther.

Take one end in each hand and separate them to get your ladder. The more sheets you can put in the tube and that you can tear, the higher your ladder will go.

Put a finger into the top of one of the tube ends and pull up the coiled paper for a couple of inches. Then pull up the paper in the other

WHEELS AND STARS

Several twenty-two and a half inch square sheets of newspaper folded into triangle shapes that look somewhat like each other are shown to your friends, but when you cut or tear the papers you make entirely different shapes out of them.

The triangles should all be folded and sharply creased before showing them.

Have them on a chair or table beside you and when ready, pick up two of them and open them out to show that they are only folded squares.

Refold and start your cutting or tearing.

When you are tearing the paper in a straight or a curved line, tear about an inch or so at a time instead of trying to give one long tear. Always tear towards you.

Your tear-out will be seen best if you hold it in front of something dark. A blackboard or a piece of dark cloth on the back of a chair will do.

You do not have to have this dark background every time. Just hold the design to one side and do not hold it in front of something white or light colored.

WHEELS

To prepare your paper so that you can tear out wheels you must first cut off a piece of the double page sheet to make the paper square.

Fold one of the sides to lie along the top edge of the sheet. Make the fold from one corner as shown here.

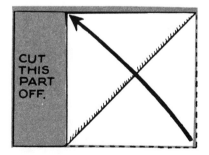

CUT THIS PART OFF.

Crease the paper where the bottom edge lies along one of the newspaper's columns. Cut or tear carefully along the crease. Unfold and you will have a square sheet of paper.

THE SHIP'S WHEEL

The drawings shown here have letters at different places to help with the folding that first has to be done. The dotted lines show where the folds are to be made. Be sure to make sharp creases on all folds.

Bring corner *D* over to *A*.

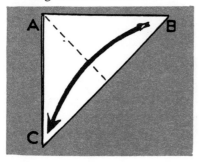

Bring corner *B* down to *C*.

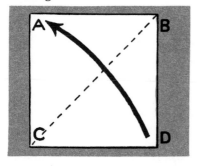

Fold down *A* and *D* to *C* and *B*.

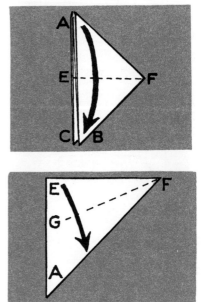

Fold corner *E* down to bring the edge *E* and *F* along the edge *A* and *F*. The paper should now resemble the sketch at top of page 133.

You may have to mark where the paper is to be torn. Use a colored pencil. Copy the pattern made here by dotted lines beginning seven inches from the corner *A* on the *AF* edge of the paper. Tear across from this seven-inch point to half an inch from the *GF* edge and then make a curved tear to *G*.

Three inches from corner *F* again tear across to half an inch from the *GF* edge and then tear along the edge for about four inches. At this point, tear back to the *AF* edge, keeping about two inches away from the first tear. When tearing the four

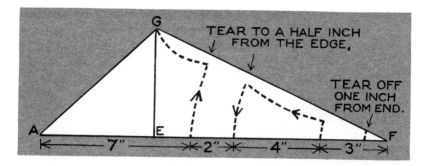

TEAR TO A HALF INCH
FROM THE EDGE.

TEAR OFF
ONE INCH
FROM END.

inches along the *GF* edge, the tearing does not have to be too straight. Tear off one inch of the corner *F* and then open out the wheel.

THE ROTARY WHEEL

Make the first two folds the same way as you did for the ship's wheel. Fold corner *D* of the square over on corner *A* and then *B* down on *C*.

With a colored pencil mark the *AB* edge eight inches down from *A* and eight and a half inches up from *B*. From these marks, *E* and *G*, rule lines to *F*.

Fold down on the *EF* line to bring the edge *AF* on the *GF* line.

Fold up the edge *BF* to have it lie along the *EF* edge. Make all of the creases sharp.

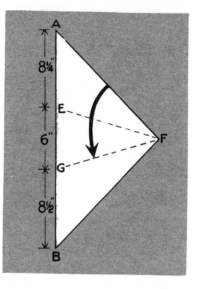

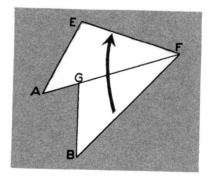

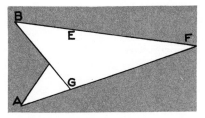

Folded and creased, the paper should look like this. Turn it over to show the *GE* edge.

Tear along the *GE* edge to get rid of the *A* and *B* pieces. Hold the paper so that the *F* corner will be pointing down.

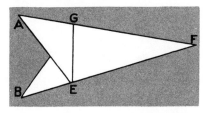

Tearing the Wheel

When the large *A* and *B* pieces have been torn off, tear out little pieces from *E* to *G*. These bits ought to be about one and a half inches deep and one and a half inches from each other. The pieces left are to be the cogs of the wheel. The end pieces at *E* and *G* ought to be smaller than the others, so that when opened out they will be the same size.

Three and a half inches down from *G* on the *GF* side, tear in a slight curve over to one inch from the *EF* side and then down at one inch from *EF* for about four inches.

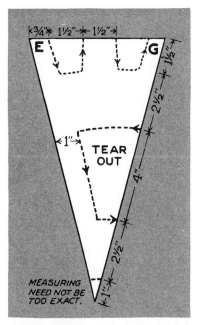

Tear out piece by tearing over to the *GF* side. Tear off about one inch of point *F*. The dotted lines show where to tear.

When the torn paper is opened out you will have a wheel like the one shown here.

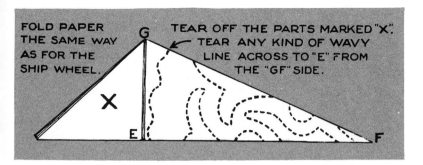

FOLD PAPER THE SAME WAY AS FOR THE SHIP WHEEL.

G

TEAR OFF THE PARTS MARKED "X". TEAR ANY KIND OF WAVY LINE ACROSS TO "E" FROM THE "GF" SIDE.

X

E

F

TABLE CENTERPIECE

Not less than one inch from the wavy line, tear out any kind of shapes you like from both the *GF* and *EF* sides, but be careful not to tear all the way across from one side to the other or have the shapes from one side too close to the shapes from the other. Tear off point *F*.

You do not have much room for a design on a piece of paper the size of the Rotary wheel, so if you can rubber cement or paste edges of several sheets or parts of them together,

you can make yourself a square big enough for a table centerpiece.

If the paper is torn as shown above, it will open out into a centerpiece like this.

TO MAKE THE BIG SQUARE

You will need a large, smooth surface on which to work.

On this surface, lay an opened double-page sheet of newspaper. Lay a second sheet on top of the first, leaving a strip about one inch wide exposed on the bottom edge of the first sheet.

If you can pin or thumbtack the sheets to the surface, do so. If not, keep the two sheets together with paper clips.

Apply paste or rubber cement to the lower edge of the top sheet and fold the uncovered edge of the lower sheet over and onto the pasted edge. Allow paste to dry. Open sheets.

Cut a third double-page spread in half, from side to side, and paste one piece on one side end of the two sheets.

To complete the big square, cut a piece to fill in the remaining corner.

ONE-CUT FIVE-POINT STAR

Make a large square from a double page of newspaper, the same as you did for the ship's wheel. Each side of the square is to be twenty-two and a half inches. Fold one of the corners over on the opposite corner so as to make a three-corner shape as shown below.

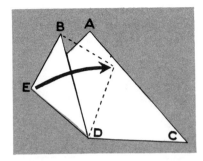

To find the center spot on the paper between the corners *B* and *C*, bring *C* over onto *B* and crease the paper where it folds at *D*. This center spot, *D*, will be sixteen inches from each of the corners.

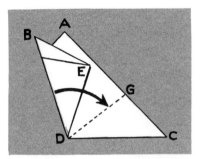

On the *BA* edge mark a spot up nine and a half inches from corner *B*, and mark another spot five and a half inches down from *A*. Draw lines from center *D* to each of the spots *E* and *F*. Fold *BD* up to lie on *FD*. Crease the fold along *ED*.

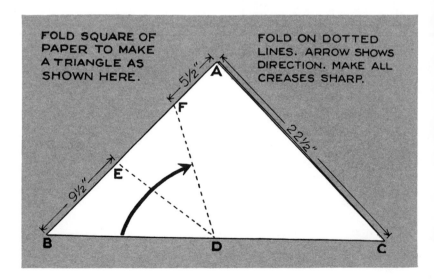

FOLD SQUARE OF PAPER TO MAKE A TRIANGLE AS SHOWN HERE.

FOLD ON DOTTED LINES. ARROW SHOWS DIRECTION. MAKE ALL CREASES SHARP.

136

Fold *E* over towards *AC* edge. Fold along *BD* and crease.

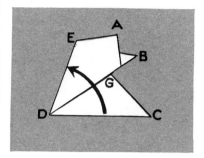

Fold *BD* edge over as shown. It should fold onto a line about half way to *DC*.

Fold *DC* edge up to lie along *DE*. *DB* is the folding line. Make all folds sharp.

Mark a spot on the *CD* edge four and a half inches up from *D*.

From this spot cut or tear a straight line to *G* on the *BD* edge.

Open out this *DG* part and you will have a five-point star. Whatever size star you make, your square of paper first should be folded into a triangle and then into five parts as shown here.

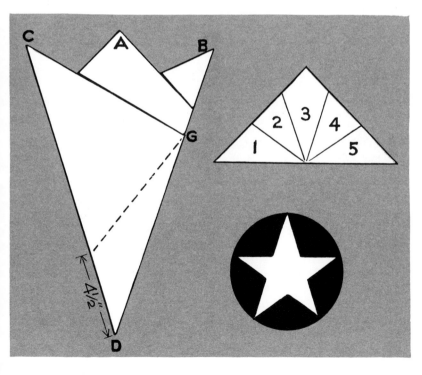

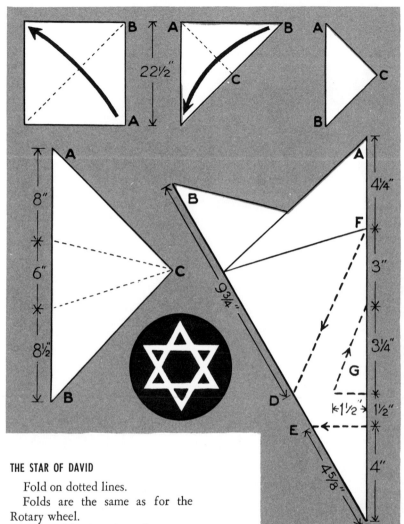

THE STAR OF DAVID

Fold on dotted lines.

Folds are the same as for the Rotary wheel.

When the paper is ready, cut or tear from F to D. Next, across to E. Then cut or tear out the small triangle G. Open out paper to get the star.

For the first few times have your den chief or Den Mother show you how to fold and mark the paper.

After a few times you ought to be able to fold, cut, or tear out the star without any marks.

ONE FROM THREE LEAVES TWO

When you have cut your big square from the double-page newspaper sheet, you will have a strip of paper left over at one of the sides. Tear this strip across to get three pieces. Keep one of these and ask two people to take the others. Make several extra pieces if you wish to have more than two people try the trick. Distribute these pieces. Tear your piece from one side as close as you can to the opposite edge. Make second tear the same way so that your paper looks as shown here.

Now tell the people who have the pieces of paper to tear them as close as they can to the edge the same as you did.

When the papers are torn ask that they be held at the top outer corners. Take your paper and show how.

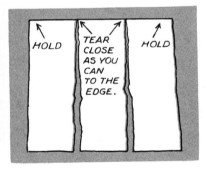

Now say, "You must not touch the middle piece with your hands, and when I count to three and say 'pull,' you are to give one pull to tear your paper into three separate pieces."

Give the signal, and the persons who pulled will find that they will be holding two pieces in one hand and one piece in the other.

Then say, "It can be done," and show how by holding the middle piece with your mouth while pulling.

Everybody will have two pieces in one hand and one in the other.

How you separate the pieces without touching the middle piece with your hands.

THE MAGIC LOOPS

Take a large double-page newspaper sheet but do not open it out as you did in the other tricks. Have it folded down the regular center fold. Two inches down from the top cut a strip across to the center fold. Cut the two pages at the same time so that when the strip is

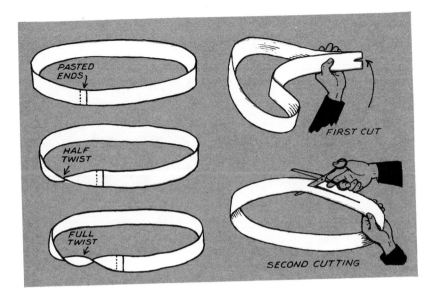

PASTED ENDS

HALF TWIST

FULL TWIST

FIRST CUT

SECOND CUTTING

No.1 LOOP DIVIDED

No.2 LOOP CUT BIG

No.3 LOOP LINKED

No.2 EXTRAS

opened out, both ends will be the same width. Cut several strips.

Paste or rubber cement the ends of a strip and join them, putting one end in about half an inch on the other end.

Give one end a half turn or twist before pasting it to the other end. Make a few extra loops like this.

Give one full turn before joining the ends of this loop. When starting to cut, begin beyond the twisted part.

Have the loops and scissors on a table. Take the loops up one at a time and hang them on your arm putting No. 2 on first. Put No. 3 on next and then No. 1.

You may hold No. 1 in your hand. Take your scissors and cut No. 1 in half along its center. The best way to start cutting is to crease the loop and cut so as to make an opening, then put one blade in the opening and cut around all the way back to the starting point. You will now have two loops.

Put these two loops on the table or around your neck and take loop No. 3 and cut it along its center the same way that you cut No. 1.

When cut, you will have two loops linked together. Now cut No. 2, and to everybody's surprise you will get only one loop and it will be a big one.

When you have cut the big loop, give one of the No. 2 extras to a friend and ask him to cut it. When he gets his big loop tell him that he could have done better. Take another of the extras, but this time

make your cut one third of the way in from the edge. As you are cutting, you will come to where you started, but your first cut will be over toward the other edge. Pass by and keep on cutting. You will come again to the starting point to finish the cut.

When opened out, you will have a large loop with a small loop linked to it.

If you are very careful and keep on bypassing the cuts, you can make a loop six or more feet long. Part of it will be two smaller linked loops.

STATIC STRIPS

Cut a few strips of newspaper each about seven inches long and one inch wide. Lay a strip on a table or on your leg and keep it in place by putting the fingertips of one hand on the end nearest you. With the fingernails of the other hand, rub vigorously on the strip eight, ten, or more times away from you (1). Pretend that you are making the strip flat with your knuckles.

Take away the hand that held the paper and pick up the strip with the hand that did the rubbing. Pick it up at the end that you were holding and give this end to someone else to hold.

Rub a second strip, pick it up and give it in the same way to the same or to another person.

Now say that you have put magic on the papers and that the two free

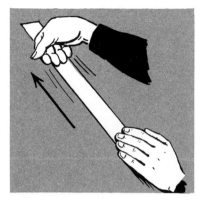

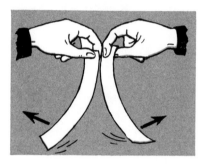

ends will not touch or stay together, no matter who tries to make them do so.

Electricity, called static, makes the papers move away from each other.

This trick works best when the weather is dry.

You may also put the static strip against a wall and it will stay there. It will stay almost any place. For fun, put it on a person's ear and say "You hear too much"; across one's eyes, "You see too much"; across one's mouth, "You talk too much."

MAGIC CARPET NO-CAN-STAY

Show a single newspaper page and say that you are going to use it as a special little magic carpet, that you are going to put it on the floor in the middle of the room, and that you want somebody to stand on it. When you have the person standing on the paper say, "It is not a magic carpet yet. I have to walk around it three times to make it magic. It will become a little more magic each time that I walk around it.

"I promise not to come near enough to touch you or the carpet with anything. When the carpet is becoming magic nobody seems to be able to stay on it. Now, if you do not take ten steps away from where you are standing before I walk around you for the third time, I will give you anything you like."

Keep as far away as you can when you are walking around. When you have made the first circle say, "Once." Go around the second time and say, "Twice." Then stop and say, "Maybe I'll walk around for the third time sometime next week."

Here is where you might wish to get away fast on a real magic carpet.

MAGIC CARPET NO-CAN-SEE

Hold out a large newspaper double-page sheet and tell your audience that you are going to use it as a magic carpet and that if anybody wants to find out its secrets he or she will have to stand on it. Say that there must be two people standing on it at the same time to make the magic work.

When you have two people who want to stand on your paper say, "When I put this down I want both of you to stand on it facing each other. Now, when you are on this magic carpet you will not be able to see each other even though your eyes are wide open. Are you ready to try? Oh yes, if either of you can prove that what I say is not true, I will give you whatever you ask for.

Put the paper down through a doorway and ask one person to go through and stand on one end of the paper. Close the door and then ask the second person to step on the inside end.

Be sure that there is no keyhole that can be seen through.

CUTOUT PUZZLES

On a piece of thin cardboard draw a three- or a six-inch square. Mark the edges and rule crosslines both ways to divide the square into nine small squares. Cut out the square

and then cut away the four small corner squares. You will now have a Red Cross shaped piece of cardboard. Use this as a pattern to make other crosses. Put the pattern on a sheet of paper and with a pencil mark its shape on the paper. Cut out this marked cross. There are to be three crosses for each person who would like to try to do the puzzles and three for yourself. Have extra crosses ready for those who want more than three. Let them try several times before you show how the puzzles are done. Do not be in a hurry.

A person having three crosses is to mark each one with no more than two straight lines so that when he or she cuts along the lines, each cross will be divided into four pieces. No cross is to be marked like either of the other two.

When one cross is cut, its four pieces are to be put together to make a square that will be the same height and width as the cross was.

Another set of four pieces is to make a square that will measure

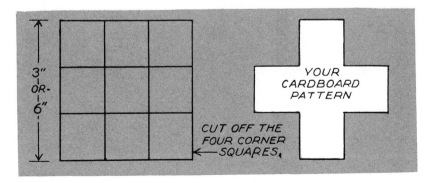

3" OR 6"

CUT OFF THE FOUR CORNER SQUARES.

YOUR CARDBOARD PATTERN

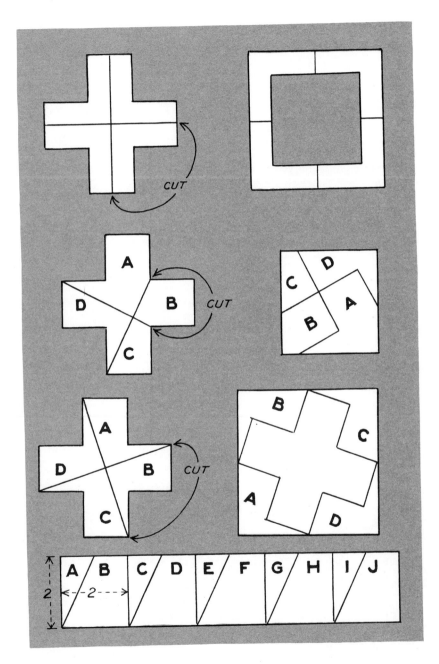

only three quarters of the cross each way.

The third set of four, when re-arranged, is to form a cross within a square.

On the opposite page are shown the crosses, the lines to be cut, and the way to put the pieces to make the squares.

1. Arrows point to the two lines to be marked and cut. The square shows how the parts make it.

2. Showing lines to be cut and the small square. The letters are just to help you arrange the pieces to make the square. They are not to be on any of the other crosses. They are only for practice.

3. The four pieces when arranged as shown leave an open space in the form of a cross. Put these pieces on a dark background to show the cross.

The Square

Mark on cardboard a strip ten inches long and two inches wide. Mark off five two-inch squares. From the lower left corner of each square draw a line to the center of its top edge as shown above. There will be ten sections marked. For practice only, put a letter in each section. Cut out the strip and cut it into the ten lettered parts.

The puzzle is to put all of the parts together to make a four-and-a-half inch square. With unmarked pieces cut and arranged as above, ask your friends to try making the square. Give them lots of time before you show how.

Either begin with the last I and

J square and put the other pieces around beginning with A at the top left corner, or start with A to make the ABC triangle, then the DE and FG triangles. To finish put in J, then I and H.

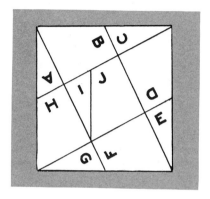

Surprise Square

Have ready a ten by one inch strip of cardboard marked across into four spaces. The spaces are to be marked in the order of one, two, three, and four inches. Ask somebody to cut the pieces apart and then put them together so as to make a square.

To show how, bring four ends of the cut pieces together as shown here. Ends of the pieces make the sides of the square which is the open space.

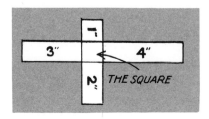

145